SECRET LOUGHTON

Michael Foley

AMBERLEY

To Anita, Lee, Chloe and Kerry, a wonderful family

First published 2017

Amberley Publishing
The Hill, Stroud
Gloucestershire, GL5 4EP

www.amberley-books.com

Copyright © Michael Foley, 2017

The right of Michael Foley to be identified as the
Author of this work has been asserted in accordance
with the Copyright, Designs and Patents Act 1988.

ISBN 978 1 4456 7444 5 (print)
ISBN 978 1 4456 7445 2 (ebook)

British Library Cataloguing in Publication Data.
A catalogue record for this book is available from the
British Library.

Origination by Amberley Publishing.
Printed in Great Britain.

Contents

Introduction

It is very difficult to write about Loughton without mentioning Epping Forest, as the forest has had a huge influence on how the town has developed and on the lives of the people of Loughton. In fact one of the earliest forms of evidence of life in the area is at Loughton Camp, an Iron Age hill fort that was built in a clearing in the forest. There is also another similar camp, Amesbury Banks, nearby. Despite rumours of Boudicca making her last stand at Amesbury, it is more likely that the forts were used as defensive positions during tribal warfare or when invaders threatened. Loughton Camp afforded views across the Roding Valley towards the Thames Estuary and Kent. Amesbury Banks had a view across the River Lea into Hertfordshire. They could both be signalled at the approach of invaders.

There seems to have been little change in the way of life in the forest, with small farming settlements thriving until the Normans arrived. With a love of hunting new laws were introduced to control the forest and officials were appointed to enforce the new laws, such as preventing raising fences and caring for the deer. There were also limits placed on how many animals the peasants could graze in the forest. There were at this time a number of villages in the forest, one of these being Loughton.

As well as the villages a number of large houses were built in the forest, as William rewarded his men with land. The process continued into the Middle Ages when the forest

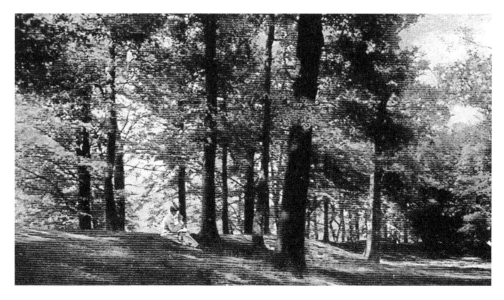

Amesbury Banks is an Iron Age hill fort near Epping that has connections with Loughton Camp. It is rumoured to be where Boudicca made her last stand.

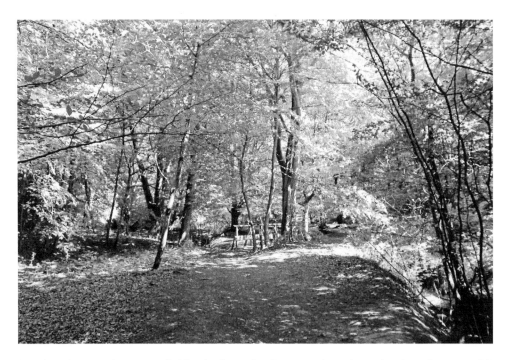

Loughton is not only surrounded by the forest but in many places it reaches into the trees with houses built into clearings.

was a favourite hunting ground for Henry VIII. At times the forest also became a place of sanctuary for those fleeing the Black Death prevalent in larger towns.

The new houses in the area meant that better roads were needed to reach them. Many of what had been old tracks through the forest were upgraded to roads during the Tudor period. Daniel Defoe in his tour of the Eastern Counties in the eighteenth century mentioned an increase in the number of handsome houses in the forest villages. They were occupied, according to him, by London citizens who could afford two houses.

As the roads improved so did the level of traffic. As the traffic increased so did the need for coaching stops and this had an influence on villages such as Loughton, which grew to meet the demand. The population of the village had been around 500 in 1763, more than 1,300 by 1841 and nearly 3,000 by 1881.

By this period it wasn't only those travelling through that came to the forest. Many of the people of London found the forest was an ideal place for a day out. Most people worked all week but on Sundays the forest would be full, and fairgrounds would be erected to attract potential visitors. Some walked, others came by horse-drawn transport and of course by this time the railways had arrived. This meant that not only could Londoners visit, but they could also live in places such as Loughton and travel up to the city every day. Of course this option was reserved for the wealthy.

Loughton developed its own identity and was seen as an area where residents were mainly from the upper classes. Of course some of the visitors came from the poorer parts of London, many brought there as a treat by charities. This often led to conflict between residents and visitors. Loughton has not always been the idyllic place it would seem to be and perhaps some of the stories in this book will uncover a less civilised Loughton and the forest around it. Loughton also dispels the myth that Essex is a flat county. Anyone who believes this has never been to Loughton.

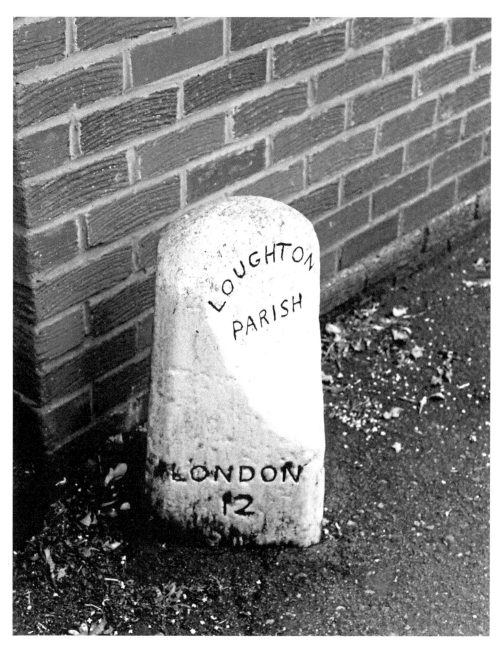

The milestone stands on the main route through Loughton and on to London through Church Hill and the High Road, which must have been the route that coaches took through the town.

1. The People of Loughton

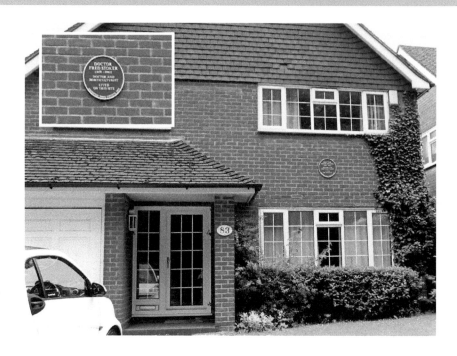

Loughton must be one of the towns with the most Blue Plaques in the country. This one is to Dr Frederick Stoker, a doctor and horticulturist who lived on Baldwin's Hill.

There seem to have been a large number of accounts of witchcraft in the Essex area, perhaps due in part to Samuel Harsnet, who became Archdeacon of Essex in 1603. Harsnet wrote a book in which he discussed the idea of witchcraft and the casting out of devils from people as nothing more than a Roman Catholic plot. This may well have been the way of thinking at the time, as Henry VIII seemed to agree with this view. A statute had been passed in 1562 that changed the death penalty for witches to a year's imprisonment. This was to change later when the punishment for witchcraft became more severe.

Loughton can claim its own witches. In 1590 Joan Mose and Agnes Mose were charged with bewitching a man to death. Joan Mose was a spinster who by wicked sorcery murdered Richard, son of Thomas Stace. Both women were found guilty and were hanged. The number of those accused of witchcraft in Essex rose sharply between 1580 and 1594.

In 1592 John Monday was charged by a churchwarden with going to a 'cunning man'. A cunning man could tell where lost or stolen goods were. Monday had to go to the court of the Archdeacon of Essex held in Romford on 3 February 1592. Even into the nineteenth century there were women who were seen to have some magical powers. Addison mentions in his book *Epping Forest* that there was a lady called Old Mother Jenkins near Epping who made her living by blessing geese.

Perhaps the earliest well-known persons in Loughton lived in the hall. Loughton Hall dated back to Tudor times and was once occupied by an Italian doctor who treated

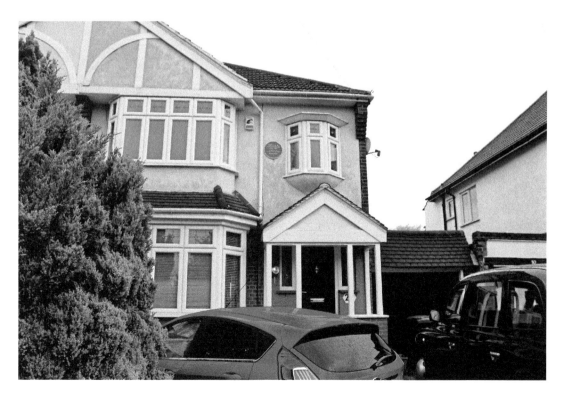

This plaque is to Donald Gillingham, the author of *Unto the Fields,* who lived in this house in Roding Road.

Henry Vlll, who often visited the house. It was then obtained by Sir Robert and Lady Mary Wroth and was rebuilt under the direction of Inigo Jones. It was completed in 1616. The house was often visited by royalty, including Elizabeth l and James l.

Loughton has a long connection with literary figures and this began with the inhabitants of Loughton Hall at the end of the Tudor period. Sir Robert and Lady Mary Wroth were the owners of the hall and one of their regular visitors was the famous playwright Ben Jonson. Lady Mary was herself a writer and is often credited as the first woman to write a published book. Despite their lofty position the couple were not happy. There were problems from the beginning of their marriage when Mary's father did not pay the dowry. Sir Robert was a gambler, philanderer and drunkard. Ben Jonson said of Lady Mary that she was married to a jealous husband. When Sir Robert died he left Lady Mary in serious debt.

Some of the residents of Loughton may have been from the upper echelons of society but this did not always mean that they behaved as gentlemen. Charles Sackville was a well- known figure in the area in the late seventeenth century. He had fought with the Duke of York in the Dutch Wars. He also wrote a song to the ladies of Whitehall that was supposed to have been written on the day before the Battle of Lowestoft, on 3 June 1665, when eighteen Dutch ships were captured. He was also a poet, often described as talented by his hangers-on who were in debt to him. Sackville was the Earl of Dorset but was known to be as wild as anyone in the Epping area, if not the country.

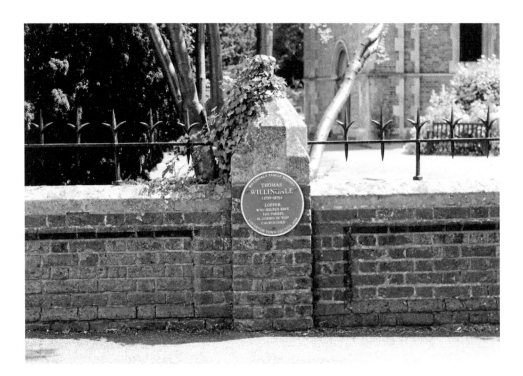

This plaque is situated on the wall of the churchyard at St John's Church. It is dedicated to Thomas Willingdale, who is buried here and who helped to save the forest.

It was said by Dr Jonson that Sackville was 'eager of the riotous and licentious pleasures that young men of high rank imagined themselves entitled to'. It was not only riotous living that he was involved in, however. On one occasion he and some friends went out after thieves but then killed an innocent man near Waltham Cross, taking his money, which they thought that he had stolen. Charged with murder, they subsequently escaped with a lesser charge of manslaughter.

Sackville also had a famous mistress, Nell Gwynn, also mistress of King Charles ll. There are various stories about who Nell described as her Charles the first. Some say it was Sackville; others say it was the king. Whatever his faults, Sackville was a very popular man in his day, well known for his generosity to the poor.

There was another woman who lived in Loughton and is remembered for her writing, although her works may not have been described as literary masterpieces. Sarah Martin wrote 'Old Mother Hubbard', the well-remembered rhyme, at the end of the eighteenth century. She is buried in the family vault in St Nicolas's churchyard.

Another writer of children's literature who lived in the area for a time was Thomas Day, who wrote the famous children's book *Sandford and Merton* in the late eighteenth century. He is perhaps better remembered for trying to train two young girls to become his perfect wife. One must wonder if Day's real-life plan had any influence on the writing of later fiction.

Day tried to train two girls in case one did not work out. He took one girl from an orphanage in Shrewsbury. Sabrina was twelve years old but proved to be unsuitable and eventually married a barrister. Lucretia, his other trainee, came from a foundling hospital

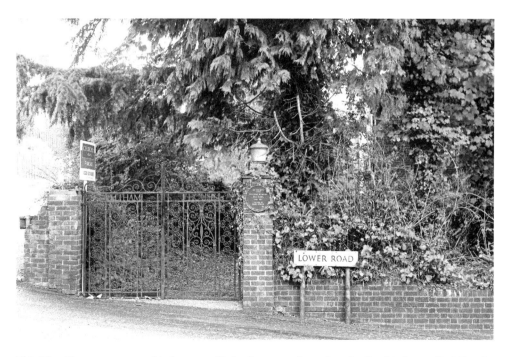

This Blue Plaque was erected in honour of John Strevens, the artist who lived in Lower Park Road.

in London and was eventually apprenticed to a milliner in Ludgate Hill and later married a draper.

A well-known military man moved to the area shortly after the Battle of Waterloo in which he had fought. General, later Field Marshal, Grosvenor rented the house that had previously been the Reindeer Inn. He planned to use it as a base to train horses to run at Newmarket.

Grosvenor employed Humphrey Repton to landscape the gardens, part of which was an enormous rabbit warren, which led to the house being known as the Warren. The Duke of Wellington was a regular visitor to the house. One of the trees in the grounds is known as Wellington's Oak as it was under this tree that he would sit and talk to Grosvenor. In a further connection with the Battle of Waterloo, Grosvenor erected a memorial in the garden to the horse he had ridden during the conflict.

The Powell family were well known in Loughton. They lived at Bench House, which was purchased in 1772. They had business interests in London and at one point owned the Whitefriars Glassworks. A later member of the family was another Baden-Powell, Robert, the founder of the Boy Scout movement, although he never lived in Loughton.

In 1802 the house became the property of David Powell, who expanded the estate by adding more land. David was a keen painter and painted a number of Essex landmarks. David was the subject of an article in *The Times* on 21 May 1832 that explained the danger of seeking shelter under a tree during a thunderstorm.

A most melancholy and fatal instance of seeking shelter under a tree during a thunder storm occurred on Tuesday last at Loughton. During the violent storm which came on in the afternoon the deceased who had been walking in his grounds was observed to go under a high elm and place himself against the body of the tree. Within a minute succeeded a most vivid flash of lightening, followed or it might be said accompanied by a tremendous burst of thunder. The electric fluid striking the tree under which Mr Powell had taken refuge and his instantaneous death was the consequence.

The newspapers of the time were not averse to horrific descriptions, and the article went on to describe how his right side was much discoloured and his clothes very much scorched. His boots were reduced to small fragments. The report then mentioned that Powell was a local magistrate and had thirteen children.

There was a further literary connection in the years between 1837 and 1841 when John Clare, who actually came from Northamptonshire, came to live in Loughton. Clare was unusual in being the son of a farm labourer but also a published poet. He had to take parish relief in 1817. His poetry was well received for a time among society in London after he was first published in 1820. He is now seen as one of the leading poets of the nineteenth century, his work reflecting concerns about the disruption of the countryside at the time.

Unfortunately his fame did not last and his later work was less well received. By 1823 he was penniless again, and despite some help from his better-off supporters he found it difficult to feed his wife and six children. He then began to display signs of mental illness and was eventually sent to Dr Allen's private asylum near High Beech.

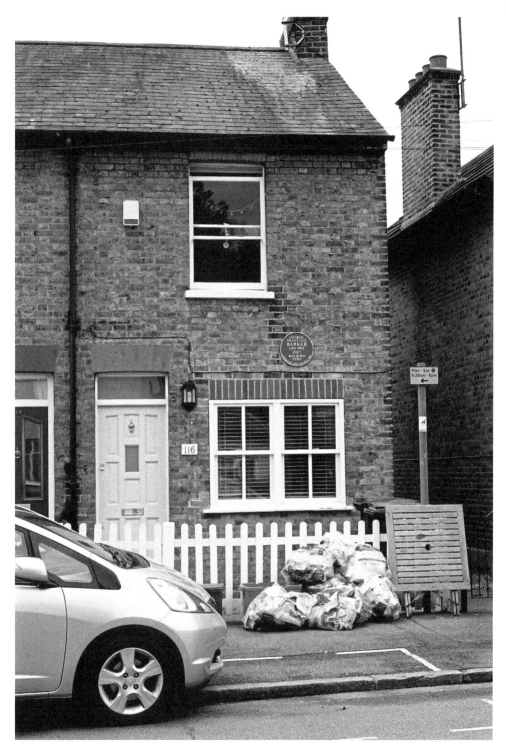

The plaque here is dedicated to George Granville Barker, the poet who lived in Forest Road in a house that looks quite modest in relation to other plaque holders.

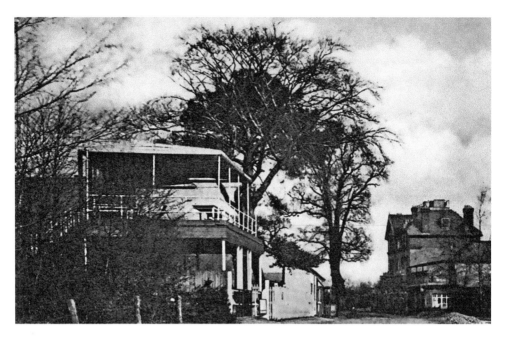

High Beech is still quite rural. It played an important role in the First World War as it was the site of a training camp.

Allen owned three houses in the area: Lippitt's Hill Lodge, Springfield House and Fairmead House.

Clare was very happy living in the area and he spent time wandering in the forest and writing about it. However, he also began to suffer from more serious mental problems, believing himself to have been Byron and Shakespeare. He later left the asylum and returned home. He was later confined to a local asylum near his home, where he eventually died.

At the same time as Clare, Tennyson also lived near High Beech. He was not as happy as Clare to live in the area, however, claiming that the only advantage to living there was that he was able to get to London more often. He met Clare and visited the asylum, where he also met Dr Allen. He later invested in a woodcarving business with Allen which failed, leaving Allen bankrupt and Tennyson much worse off than he had been.

One of the most well-known literary connections with the area is of course in Dickens's *Barnaby Rudge*. It is thought that Dickens was thinking of the King's Head, Chigwell when he mentioned the Maypole at Chigwell Row in the book, which was published in 1841, five years after Loughton Hall burnt down. According to a local story, during the fire the butler was woken by the bell in the library, which was set ringing by falling masonry – an event similar to a passage in *Barnaby Rudge*. According to press reports, however, this was not what had happened when the hall caught fire. Smoke was discovered in the library by a maid.

It wasn't only celebrities that were reported in the press. *The Times* of 13 November 1876 reported on the 800th anniversary of lopping rights in the forest. Problems were to arise when the forest was placed under the control of the Corporation of London. It said

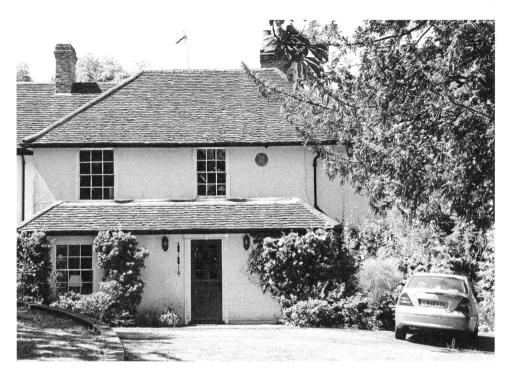

The plaque on the Meads on Church Hill is dedicated to Millais Culpin, a medical psychologist who lived there.

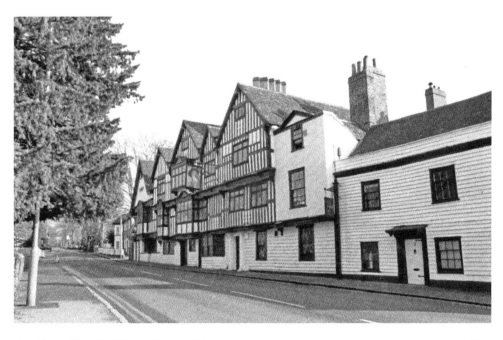

The King's Head in Chigwell is a well-known public house in the area and was once the local for those serving at RAF Chigwell.

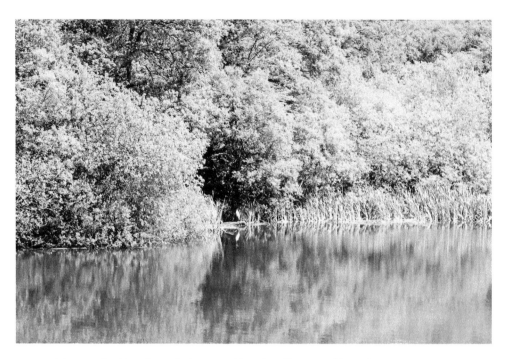

A peaceful view of Baldwin's Pond close to Baldwin's Hill. Just visible in the centre of the image is a heron standing on the bank.

that at midnight the population of Loughton assembled at the Robin Hood Hotel, High Beech, where they were served with venison from a deer hunted at Easter. At midnight the people were led by a procession of Metropolitan Police officers mounted and on foot to Staples Hill, where the boughs were cut.

Another famous writer who once lived in Loughton was Rudyard Kipling, although this was as a boy before he became the well-remembered author. Kipling had been at a school at Southsea for six years. It was a school for children whose parents were in India. Kipling got on well with the schoolmaster, an ex-naval man. His wife, however, would beat the children regularly.

Eventually his mother returned from India and took him away from the school. He lived with a farmer on Goldings Hill. He made friends with everyone and ran wild in the forest. He even became friends with a gypsy horse seller. Kipling was also visited by his cousin, the young Stanley Baldwin, and they played together on an island in Goldings Hill Pond.

On Pole Hill once stood a small hut that was used by Vyvyan Richards, a friend of T.E. Lawrence. Lawrence would visit his friend at the hut and they planned to set up a printing press where they could publish Lawrence's books. Lawrence later bought the land the hut stood on and together they planned to build a hall. There is little doubt that the forest had woven its spell on Lawrence, as it had other literary figures. However, the hall was never built and Lawrence never did live there.

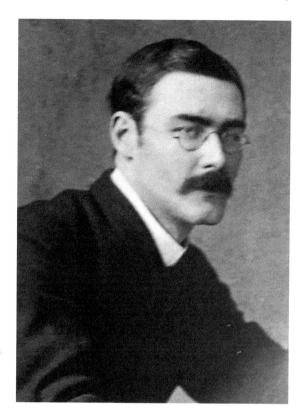

Rudyard Kipling lived in Loughton as a boy after being removed from a school where he was regularly beaten.

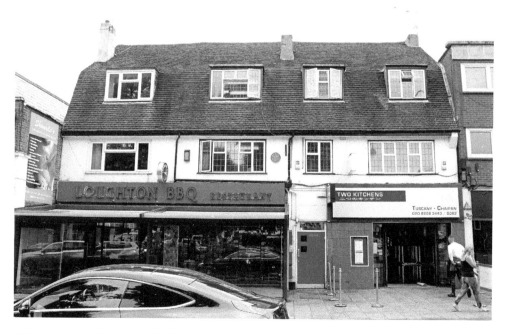

This shop in High Road with the plaque was once a bookshop owned by the author, jurist and historian Sir William Addison.

There were many stories of strange cures by chemists and doctors in the nineteenth century, many of which did more harm than good. There was an event in June 1898, however, that led to such a miraculous cure that it was reported in newspapers throughout the country. Miss Busbridge lived in Alfred's Road, Buckhurst Hill and was described as a tall, good-looking young lady of twenty-five years of age. She was thought to have been ill for two years and had been taken to London hospitals until she 'wished to be carried to her grave'. Five doctors gave her up as a hopeless case. Her lungs were seriously affected and her symptoms were seen as evidence of consumption.

Consumption was a disease that in the nineteenth century almost always led to death. Miss Busbridge spent some time in Devon hoping the air there would improve her condition, but she came back worse and had to be carried home from the train. Her sister was then advised to get her a box of Dr Williams' Pink Pills for Pale People. She took them to please her sister.

After six months of taking the pills Miss Busbridge was able to walk unaided. She gained 30lbs in weight. It was claimed in a report in *The Times* that these pills had cured thousands of people of anaemia, rheumatism, eczema and even St Vitus's Dance. The report went on to say that only Dr Williams' Pink Pills worked; other 'pink pills' were useless copies.

The newspapers of the time were full of amazing cures like the pink pills, which had begun life in Canada but became common in all parts of the Empire by the late nineteenth century. They were in fact a type of iron pill, so may have had some effect on certain illnesses or conditions.

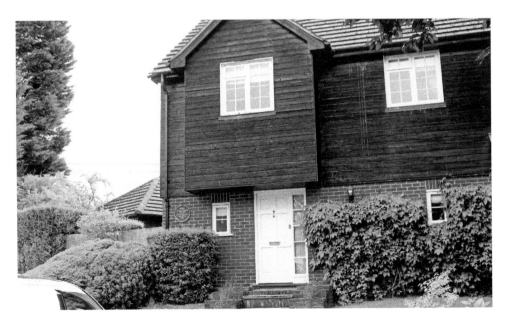

Historian William Chapman Waller lived in Ash Green, but this house has been built on the garden of his old home and is now called Waller Hoppit.

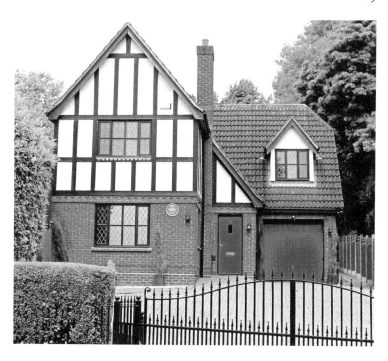

The plaque commemorates Arthur Morrison, the author who lived in Salcombe House, which once stood on this part of High Road.

It seems that despite Loughton being a lure to writers, not all were inspired by the forest. W.W. Jacobs lived at The Outlook, Park Hill. He also owned Feltham House, Goldings Hill, which has a Blue Plaque commemorating him. When asked if the view from his windows of the forest inspired him he said that he always wrote facing a blank wall. Jacobs mainly wrote humorous stories but is perhaps best remembered for his horror story *The Monkey's Paw*. The fictional village of Claybury in many of his stories is thought to be Loughton.

There have been numerous writers living in Loughton over the years but it was not only literary men who resided here. Jacob Epstein was an American who later took British citizenship. He lived at both No. 49 and No. 50 Baldwin's Hill and there is a Blue Plaque on No. 50. Epstein was a sculptor and a painter and when he produced a number of nude statues – which stand on what is now Zimbabwe House in the Strand – they were seen as shocking to Edwardian society.

Epstein did much of his work at his homes in Loughton, and there is little doubt that the forest was an inspiration to him. He was often seen wandering among the trees and said of one of his best-known works, 'The Visitation', that he would have liked this figure to remain standing above the trees. He also painted more than a hundred watercolours of the forest.

It would seem that Loughton has long been the home of the more affluent members of society. There is no doubt that there were also some people from the lower classes residing there as well, but they were usually servants of the wealthy.

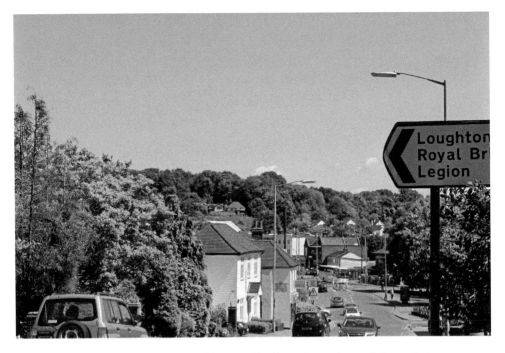

A view from Church Hill towards Goldings Hill, where the main road through the town was extended towards Epping in the past, but it was still a difficult route for coaches.

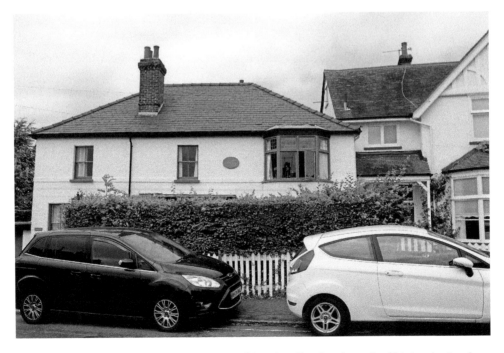

Sir Jacob Epstein, sculptor and artist, lived in Baldwin's Hill and took much of his inspiration from the surrounding forest. His plaque here is stone rather than blue.

When something went wrong among the poor of the town there was not always a great deal done for them. At the end of 1876 a man living in what was described as a small house in the most densely populated part of Loughton was visited by his grown-up son, who lived in London. It seems that the son was not feeling well and thought that a few days in the country would improve his symptoms. He went to the doctor, who told him to go home and then visited him there to inform him that he had smallpox.

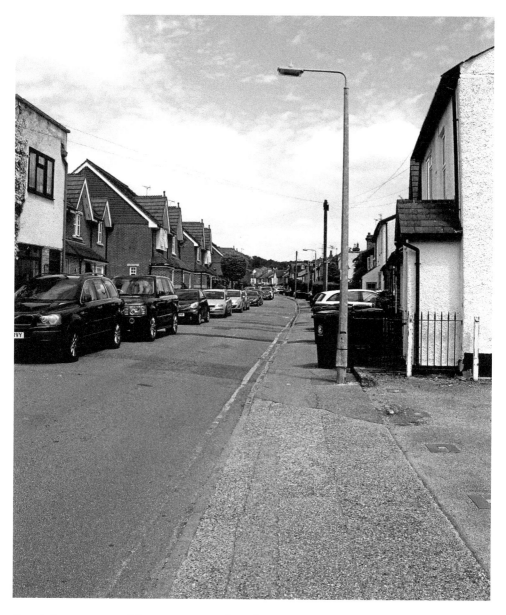

Smarts Lane was one of the poorer areas of Loughton, it was where the rich recruited their staff. Many of the older small houses have survived.

The man's father had a wife and three children also living in the house. The father went to the doctor to see about having his son taken into hospital. He was referred to the relieving officer, who could do nothing but refer him to the officer of the board of guardians at Epping. The father then walked to Epping, which was a 10-mile journey (including his return). He was told that the medical officer would visit his son that afternoon.

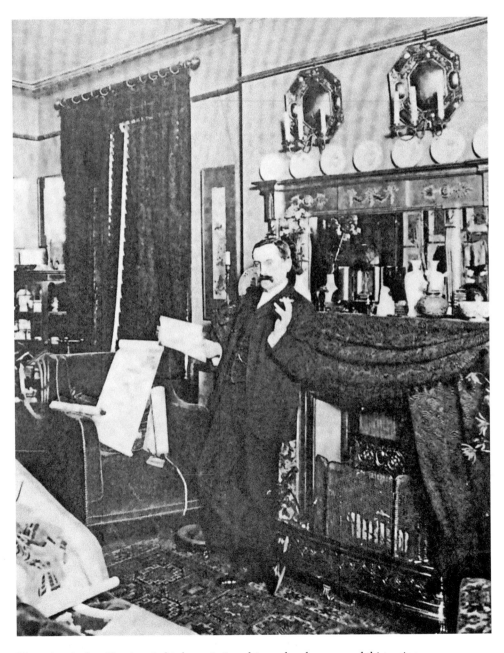

The writer Arthur Morrison in his home in Loughton, when he was aged thirty-nine.

No one turned up, and the father received a letter the next day saying nothing could be done until the board met on the Friday. After the meeting the officer of the board returned to Loughton to inform him that every place was full and even if it wasn't the man was now too far gone to be moved. It was then reported that other cases of smallpox had been reported in the village where there had been none before.

In a letter to *The Times* a resident of Loughton asked if there was no machinery available to the Board of the Poor and to the Board of Health to prevent the outbreak of such a disease due to the visit of a young man to a country village, especially when the Board of Guardians of the Union embraced several large parishes.

There was an interesting report in *The Times* in July 1878 which provided a good example of the attitude towards the less well-off members of society by those in loftier positions. It was in relation to rail travel and also has some relevance to rail travel today, especially in London. An excursionist had taken a third-class return journey to Loughton on a bank holiday. On his return at night he found that the third-class carriages had no lights and that it was so crowded that several people had to stand.

In addition to this, during the journey some of the passengers became quarrelsome and began to fight. The passenger then brought an action against the rail company for not providing reasonable accommodation. Mr Justice Manisty decided in favour of the company and when giving judgement remarked that a third-class excursionist on a bank holiday had no right to expect lights or other accommodation to be provided for him.

It wasn't only the better-off who moved to the area in the nineteenth century, however. Poorer people built themselves cottages on the edge of the forest. They would then create

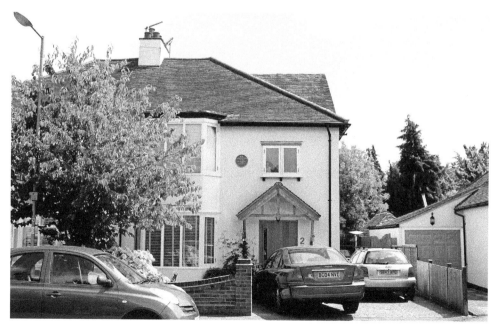

This plaque commemorates Ron Greenwood, manager of West Ham United and later the England national football team.

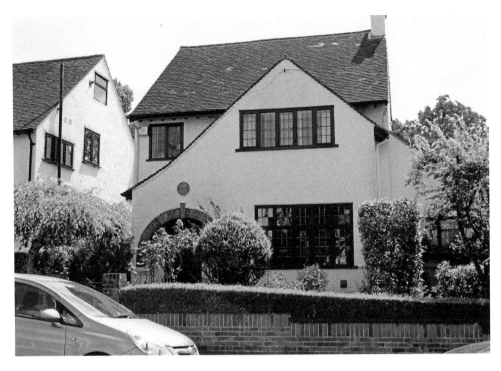

Architect Sir Frank Baines lived in this house at The Uplands, off Church Hill.

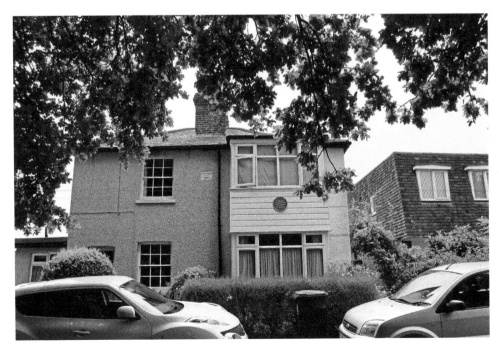

Both Muriel and Doris Lester lived in this house in Baldwin's Hill. They were peace campaigners and philanthropists.

a garden by using bramble plants as a fence, and they would cut this back from the inside while letting it spread on the outside, increasing the size of the land they had enclosed. This was often land that belonged to the local lord. The enclosures continued, so that between 1850 and 1870 the size of what had been Epping Forest declined by half, from 6,000 acres to 3,000.

One of the worst offenders was the Revd John Whitaker Maitland, who had enclosed a lot of land at Loughton. In 1865 Maitland tried to take a man called Thomas Willingale to court for damaging the forest. There had been a rule that men were allowed to cut wood in the forest during the winter. Willingale was offered support in his court case by Sir Thomas Fowell Buxton, who disagreed with Maitland enclosing so much land.

Edward North Buxton of Woodford was a member of the Commons Preservation Society, which had already stopped some enclosures. Edward was Sir Buxton's brother. The society supported the City of London Corporation in taking legal action against any further enclosures and in 1874 they were successful. All forest land enclosed after 1851 was returned to the forest if it had not been built on. In 1878 the City of London Corporation became conservators to the forest and it was saved for public use.

Queen Victoria visited Chingford in 1882 to announce that the forest had been saved for the people. The schoolchildren of Loughton and other nearby areas were all given a holiday and taken to see the Queen.

This new ruling may have pleased those living in London and the surrounding areas but not everyone in Loughton was happy. Locals had been used to taking what wood they needed from the forest to keep them warm in the winter. This all ended when the forest

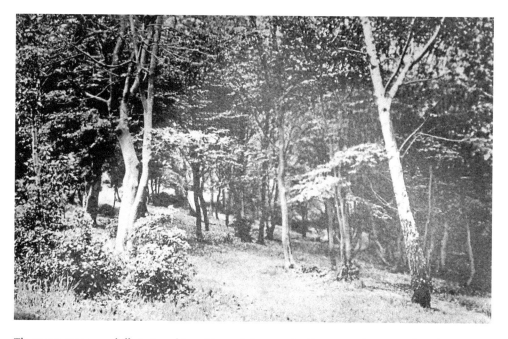

There are numerous hills in Loughton. Many of them are built upon and some such as this one are still part of the forest.

was bought by the Corporation of London. The money from the sale was used to build Lopping Hall, but what was left over was distributed to the older residents of the area.

Being a quiet, rural area at this time one would expect it not to have suffered from some of the problems more common in nearby London. One local resident, however, remembered being shown her grandmother's grave in the late nineteenth century. She was told that when her mother was buried her grandfather and a neighbour would watch over the grave every night for two weeks to ensure that the bodysnatchers did not get her.

The end of the nineteenth century was to see a further development as thousands of children from London began to arrive in the area. This was organised by Sir Arthur Pearson, the man responsible for *Pearson's Weekly* and the Ragged School Union. Pearson set up a Fresh Air Fund; it cost 9*d* to send each child by train from London to Snaresbrook, and then they would walk to Wanstead Flats.

The problem with the trips was that temporary accommodation had to be put up and taken down each day. Permanent accommodation was eventually found in Loughton. The Melbourne Retreat in Staples Road had been used as a place to offer refreshments to visitors of the area. The Ragged School Union then bought it as a permanent venue for the children.

There were problems, however. Loughton was still mainly occupied by more well-to-do members of society. Those who lived in more humble accommodation normally were often servants for these people. Having crowds of children from the poorer areas of

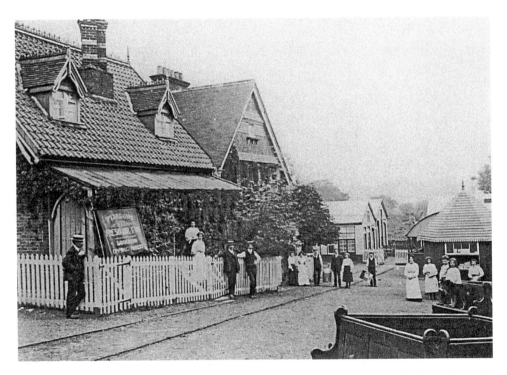

Shaftesbury Retreat, where children from all over London were brought to spend a day or longer in the forest.

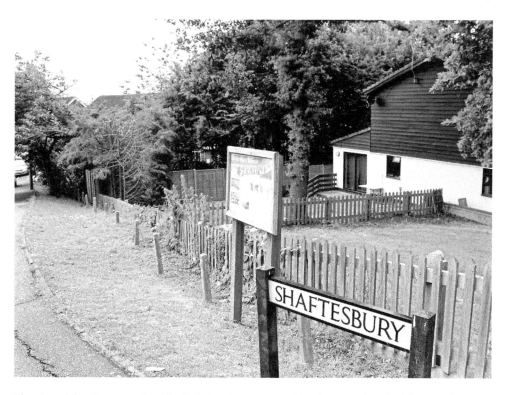

The site of the Retreat today. The building has gone and has been replaced with a new housing estate, but is remembered in the name of the road.

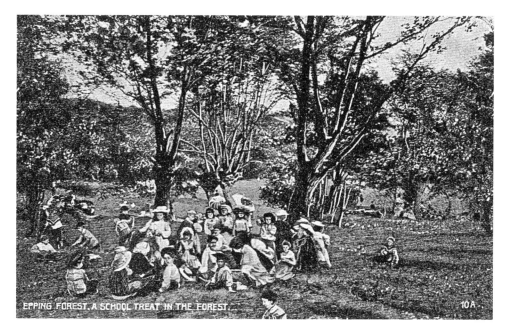

Children visiting the forest on a school trip. They were not always popular with locals.

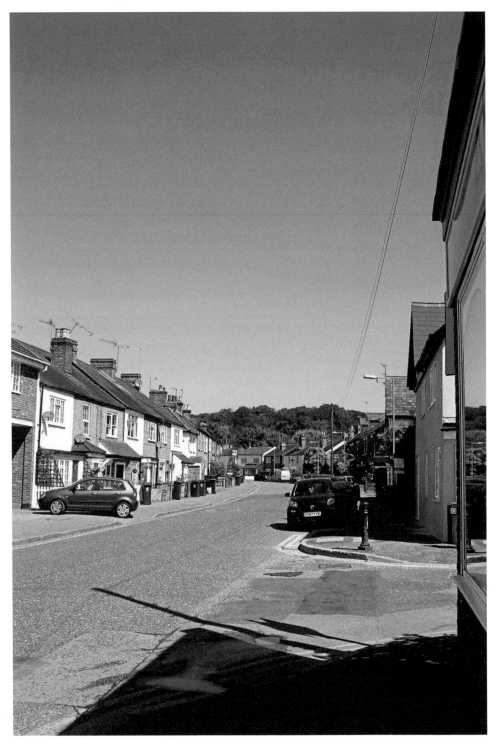

Forest Road may be one of the lesser grand roads in Loughton but it has a great view of the forest at its far end.

London arriving in their town was not something the rich were very happy about – the children were dirty and they were often far from polite.

There were complaints by locals of the children loitering in the streets, robbing locals' gardens, leaving litter and swimming in the reservoir. A water cart would follow the children through the streets as they arrived to clean the road behind them. The route they took had to vary; they would walk from the station to the Retreat along Forest Road. They would then return by Smarts Lane to avoid upsetting those in Forest Road twice in the same day.

It is doubtful if the use of coaches to bring visitors on tours of the forest caused such unrest among local residents as the arrival of children from the East End did. In May 1893 there was a report in *The Times* on coaching in Epping Forest. It seems that the coaching season began in May, with several coaches taking people on excursions to various parts of the country.

The coach was called the *Telegraph* and started from the Royal Forest Hotel in Chingford and drove through what was described as delightful country for two and a half to three hours. The route took in Fairmead Plain, Amesbury Banks and Staples Hill, then along Loughton Road to Chigwell. The cost was four or five shillings for the box seat, so the people taking the trip would not have been the poorest of the visitors to Loughton.

The coach did two trips per day and also picked up from Chingford station. When one thinks of coaches in the Victorian period they tend to be ones carrying passengers from place to place rather than taking them on excursions.

It wasn't only children on excursions annoying the local residents. In April 1912 a travelling showman found himself in Stratford Court for permitting a steam organ to be played on

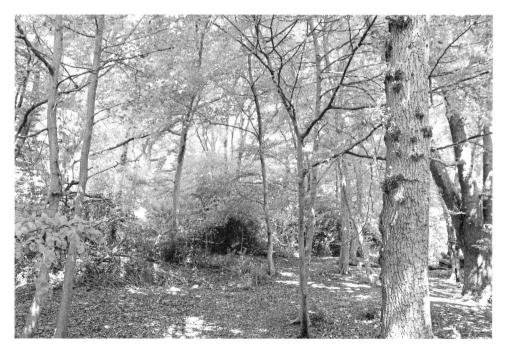

This photograph shows the view of the forest from Staples Road, which runs from the site of the old Shaftesbury Retreat to York Hill.

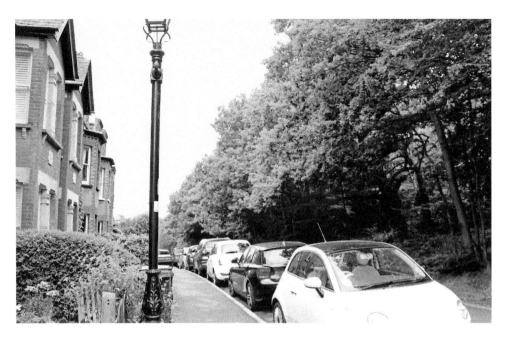

Staples Road, showing houses on one side of the road and the forest on the other.

land adjoining the highway to the annoyance of the residents of Church Hill. Theodore Ridley Burnet, a schoolteacher of Goldings Park, said that the organ, which was near the Plume of Feathers public house, had been played on the previous Saturday from six until eleven o'clock in the evening. It was a great nuisance and got on the nerves of his wife, who was in delicate health.

Another local resident, Mr W.W. Jacobs, an author, said that he heard the organ and that if he wanted any quiet he could not occupy the rooms on the side of the house nearest to the instrument. He claimed that on the Saturday night the organ had played for six hours. The showman was fined twenty shillings.

Up until the First World War it was not unusual to see gentlemen in top hats and morning suits being carried to the station in horse-drawn cabs. Once there they would be escorted to first-class carriages by the stationmaster. This was in the pre-electric Central Line days when the engines of the Great Eastern and later the London & North Eastern Railways were driven by steam.

No doubt the remuneration that these men received far exceeded the eighteen shillings a week that the cab drivers earned, waiting in the cabman's shelter until the last train from London had arrived. They would be hoping that the fire brigade from the fire station at the top of Station Road would not be called out as the horses that pulled the cabs doubled as the pulling power for the fire engine.

There were times when being in service in Loughton had its perks. Phyllhaven House was on Alderton Hill but the name has changed since it was called this in the early twentieth century. The cook at the house was called Kate and while the owners of the house spent Christmas in Madeira she would invite her brother's family, who lived in

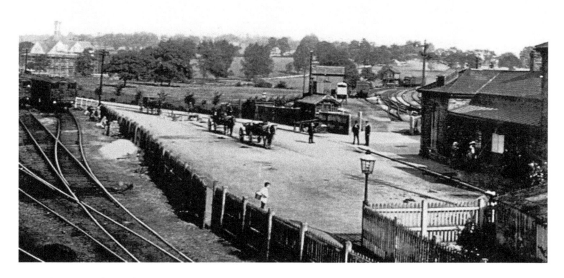

The original Loughton station opened in 1856 and was near Lopping Hall and surrounded by large goods yards. A new station was built in 1865 when the line was extended to Epping.

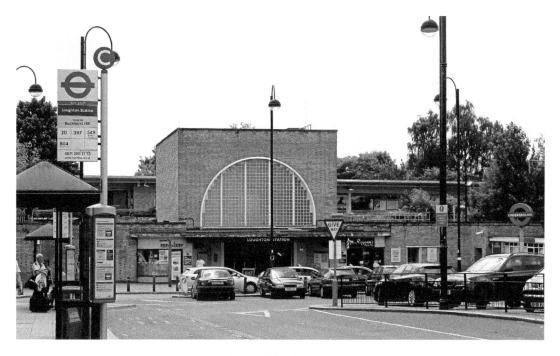

The present station was built in 1940 to be used for the new Central Line that took over from the old British Rail Line.

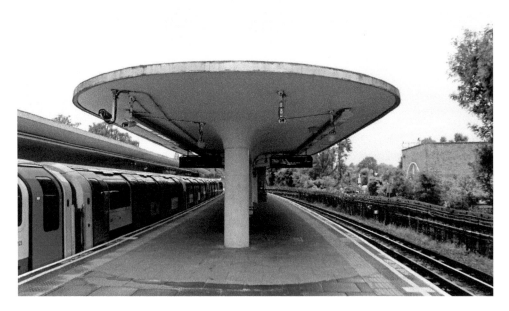

The station is a Grade ll-listed building and, as can be seen, the design of the platform coverings is very unusual.

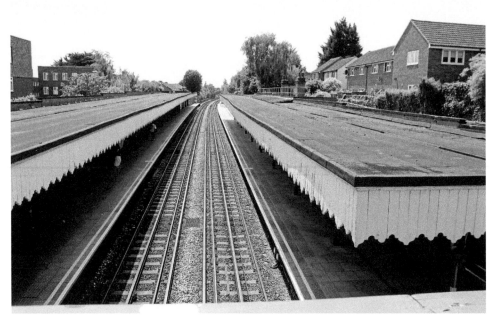

Buckhurst Hill station opened in 1856 and must be very similar to what the original Loughton station looked like.

Smarts Lane, to Christmas dinner at the house she worked in. As Smarts Lane was one of the poorer streets in the town the difference must have been evident to all of them. While there the children would be allowed to use the bath, which was a luxury as they normally had to use a tin bath at home. Up until 1920 Smarts Lane was known as the humblest road in the village and consisted of old boarded cottages and brick ones that were similar to those found in the poorer parts of London.

Kate would also take her nephews to Christmas Day Mass at St Mary's Church. The gentry would sit in rented pews while the rest of those present would sit in the free pews, including the orphan girls from St Ethelberga's Home, who all wore straw hats.

The people of Loughton were privileged to listen to Winston Churchill and find themselves involved in international affairs in October 1924, when he gave a speech at a large meeting in Loughton and gave some evidence of his long-held animosity towards the Russians – Churchill was critical of the British Socialists and their solidarity with Russia.

Churchill saw his selection as the candidate for Epping as a move that put country before party and described how the Russians had designs on Britain, as exposed by the Foreign Office. He accused Ramsay MacDonald of having a sense of comradeship with the 'filthy butchers of Moscow'.

Churchill was no doubt referring to the recognition of the Soviet Union by the Labour government in 1924 and the publication of the 'Zinoviev Letter' – Zinoviev being the head of the Communist International in Moscow – in the *Daily Mail*. The letter stated that recognition of the Soviet Union would lead to the radicalisation of the British working class. The letter was later deemed a forgery but was a useful tool in the Conservative election programme.

Churchill went on to say that he hoped the electors would show by their votes their condemnation of the Russian and German doctrine and have a government in power that was English and British in its character and which, of course, would result in his own return to the House of Commons.

It seems that Churchill was a popular speaker in Loughton as he returned again in October 1925. This time he was mainly concerned about farmers and how they should have little governmental interference. He also went on to discuss problems with the unions and how the country was to be governed under the old constitution or by some form of Soviet. Churchill had a hatred of anything resembling Communism, a view no doubt supported by the residents of Loughton.

Camps for unemployed men were established in the area in the 1930s. There was a Pathé film made about the camps. They were called the Fellowship Holiday Camps and were for men who were unemployed in London. They could apply through their social service centre, the labour exchange or directly to the mayor of the area they lived in. Then, for three shillings and sixpenc, they could have a week's holiday.

The Pathé film showed rows of bell tents which together resembled something like an army camp. A man blew a whistle and the men came out, throwing their bedding out with them. They were then shown doing exercises and swimming in the River Lea. A group then danced to a man playing the piano while the rest watched, singing 'I do like to be beside the seaside'.

The Times reported on this camp in September 1933. The chairman of the camp was Colonel Mallinson and the camp commandant was Captain Abley. The report said that

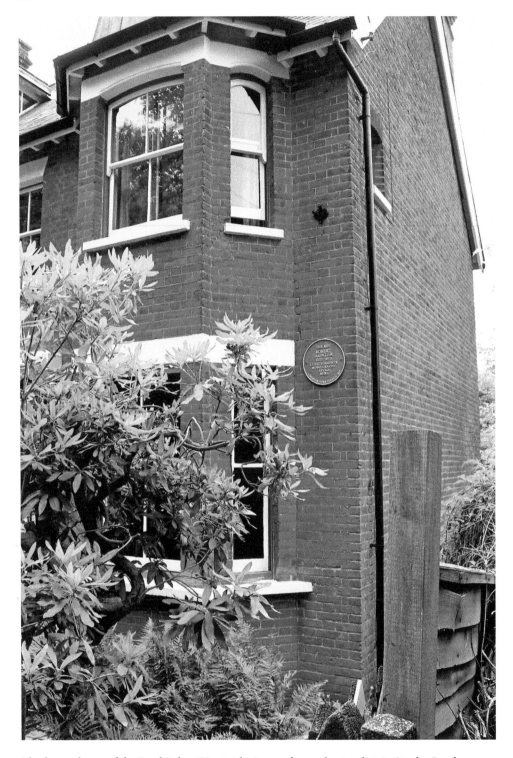

The former home of the Revd Robert Hunter, lexicographer and naturalist, in Staples Road.

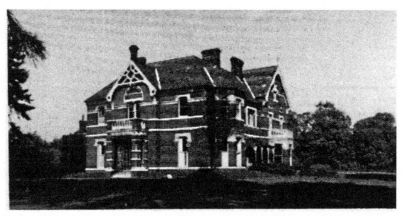
An advertisement for the sale of a large house. Many of the large houses in Loughton were sold off with the grounds used for more modern building.

men came from all over London, recommended by various charities. The numbers rose from twenty men a week to over a hundred.

Colonel Mallinson said that it was most amazing that so many men had come and that there had been no unfortunate incidents. It had been hard convincing men to come as they were unwilling to believe that anyone in the world wanted to help them.

The camps had their own barber, a bootmaker and first-aid station. The activities included boating, swimming, bowls, football and cricket. Some men even had flying lessons at the local aerodrome. It was said that the men returned from the camps with renewed confidence and were able to get jobs because of this.

The visit by children from the East End continued up until the Second World War. The following is a quote from the May 1935 edition of *Pearson's Weekly*: 'We got up very early in the morning and crept from the tent down into the valley. The boys were from the city and not accustomed to country ways, not one of them had been outside London. The sun rose higher until the great red disc was peeping over the horizon.' One of the boys then said, 'I say sir isn't god wonderful.' The article then went on to ask for one and threepence to send a child to the country for a day, or a pound, which would pay for a fortnight's holiday.

By the time the previous article had been published the Ragged School Union had become the Shaftsbury Society and had purchased the old National School in Staples Road. It was called Ashley Camp House and it was used for longer holidays for children. The trips came to an end during the Second World War and did not recommence after the conflict.

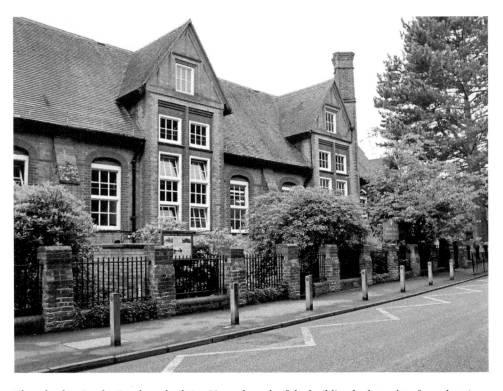

The school in Staples Road was built in 1887 and much of the building looks to date from that time.

2. Schools and Buildings

It may have been some years before there were recognised schools in Loughton, but in 1832 there was a strange story about a boarding school in the town run by a Mr Stevens. It concerned the children of a Lieutenant Chambers of the Royal Navy who had died during the Battle of Camperdown in 1797. There were four Chambers children, three girls and one boy, all of whom were orphaned.

The oldest child received forty shillings per annum and the other children ten shillings per annum from the Admiralty. One of the sisters was, according to *The Times*, afflicted with imbecility. The eldest child, Miss Chambers, therefore found a place at a boarding school in Loughton for the boy. It was run by Mr Stevens, who had agreed to educate the child for £18 per annum.

After four months at the school Mr Stevens sent Miss Chambers a bill for £8 14s 9d, which she struggled to pay and so sent £7 instead. Four months later Mr Stevens sent another bill for £13 17s. She wrote to remind Mr Stevens of their agreement and sent 5s to buy the boy a pair of shoes.

The schoolmaster replied threatening legal action if she did not pay and then took the 5s off the bill. He then sent the boy home without any shoes and with his clothes in a box, which was not fastened and meant that most of his clothes were stolen. The magistrate said that he could not stop Mr Stevens from suing her for the money he said she owed but it was doubtful that under law she would have to pay it.

A few weeks after the case was reported in *The Times* a letter appeared in the newspaper from Mr Stevens, claiming that the statements made by Miss Chambers were unfounded and that since the article had appeared he had been much annoyed by anonymous scribblers who he deemed were being injurious to his professional character. It was signed J.W. Stevens, schoolmaster, Loughton.

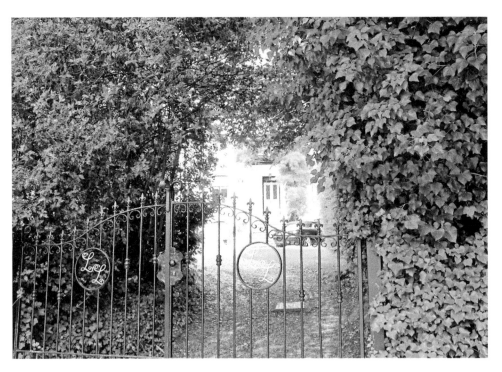

Loughton Lodge was once the home of Mary Anne Clarke, the mistress of Prince Frederick, Duke of York and Albany. The lodge stands in Steeds Way.

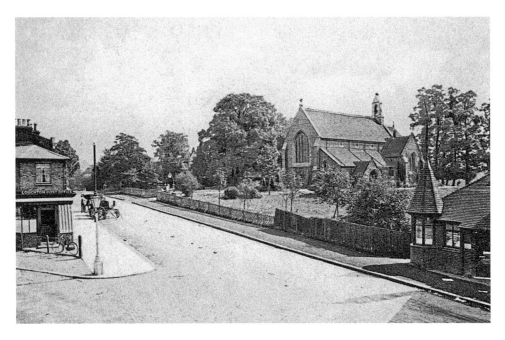

St Mary's Church was built in 1872 to provide for a second parish in Loughton. It was built near the station, where most of the people lived.

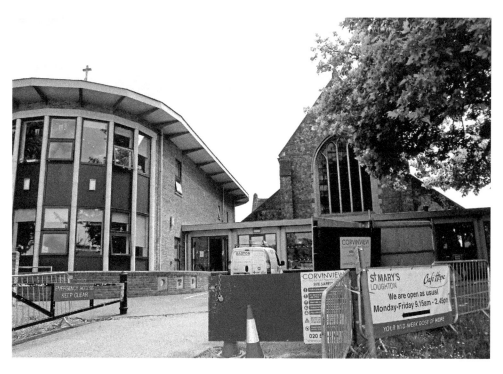

The photograph of St Mary's Church shows how much work has been done to add to the older building.

One of the most important buildings in Loughton suffered a terrible fate on 11 December 1836 when it was destroyed by fire. At the time Loughton Hall was owned by William Whittaker Maitland, who was the High Sheriff of Essex. Only the east wing survived and according to *The Times* property amounting to between £20,000 and £30,000 was lost.

There was a rumour that a butler was woken by the bell in the library as something fell onto it, but according to *The Times* one of the female servants saw smoke and knowing that there was no fire alight at the time raised the alarm. The fire engine arrived soon after, as did many of the locals wanting to help. Two locals even rode to London to raise the London fire engines in Watling Street. Two engines from London then attended but could do no more to save the west wing of the building.

It was estimated that fifty rooms were destroyed or damaged plus 10,000 valuable books, most of the furniture and between 7,000 and 8,000 bottles of wine. The fire engines carried on working the next day using water from nearby ponds and supported by a large number of local people. The building was insured by the Imperial Fire Office and the owner of the hall, Mr Maitland, was himself a director of the insurance company.

It had been the custom since the previous owner of the hall, his aunt, Mrs Whittaker, to give every labourer living on the estate 7lbs of beef and bread and potatoes at Christmas, as well as some money calculated in relation to the number of persons in the family. The estate actually covered all of Loughton and a great deal of land around it as

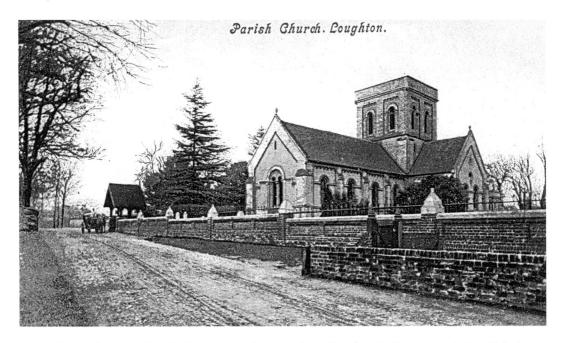

Parish Church. Loughton.

Although the original parish church in Loughton stood near Loughton Hall, it was partly demolished after St John's was built in 1846.

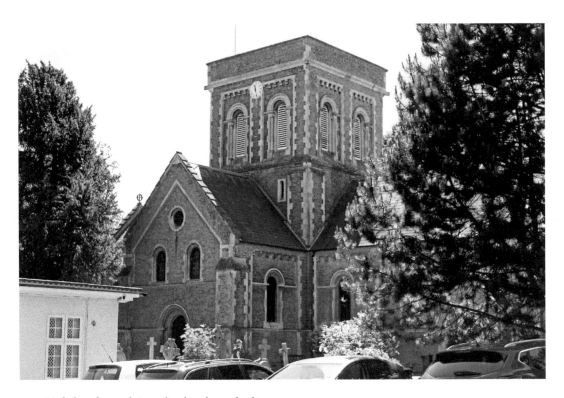

Little has changed since the church was built.

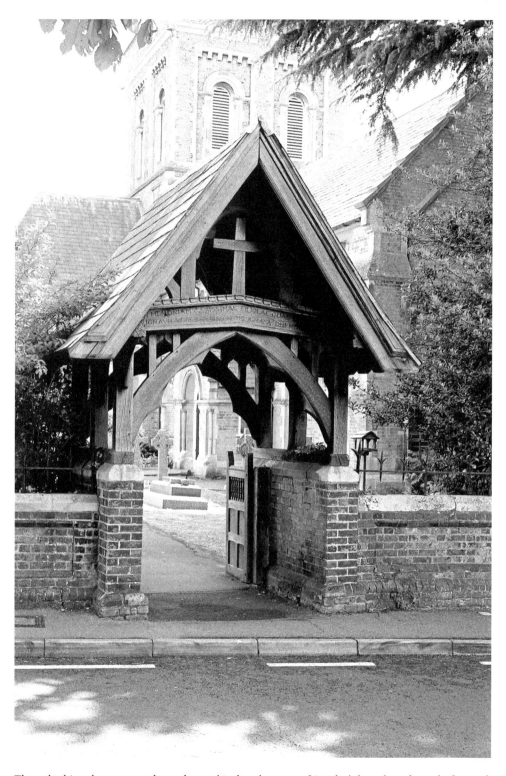

The only thing that seems to have changed is that the gates of St John's have been brought forward.

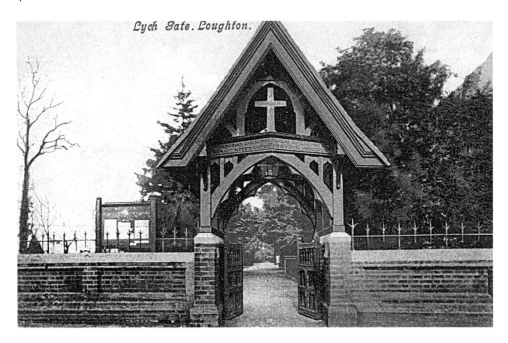

Lych Gate. Loughton.

The lychgate at St John's Church was originally a shelter for those bringing bodies to be buried. Lych is derived from the old English 'lich', meaning corpse.

well. The locals understandably were worried that the Christmas bounty would not be forthcoming due to the losses suffered by Mr Maitland. However, instead of giving the local people their normal amount of food that year Mr Maitland actually doubled the amount. He said that when the hall had been on fire up to 200 of his humble neighbours had come to his assistance. He said that they worked hard and that not one of them was a thief. He also extended his hospitality to the firemen working at the hall.

The hall was rebuilt in 1878 when it was owned by the Maitland family. The hall was taken over by the army during the Second World War and purchased by the council afterwards. It is now a residential home for the elderly.

Humphrey Repton was a man with connections to Loughton, and he was worried about the fever for fast travel that was sweeping the country in the eighteenth century, leading to the carving up of the English countryside by straight roads, which was happening in the areas surrounding Loughton too. There were also two steep hills that needed to be reduced for coaches. These were at the north and south end of Loughton – Goldings at the north and Buckhurst Hill at the south. Eventually, after many failed plans, it was decided to bypass Loughton altogether and build a road from Woodford to the Wake Arms.

Buildings in Loughton did not always remain in the same hands or for the same use. Little Standing began life as a Crown building used as a keeper's lodge. It was later rebuilt and became the Reindeer Inn. It was then bought and turned into a country house. It was purchased by General (later Field Marshal) Grosvenor in 1815, and he used it to train horses to race at Newmarket.

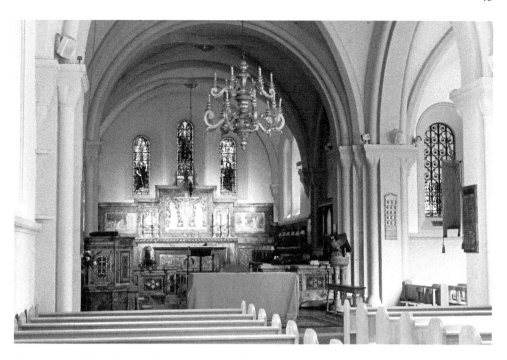

The interior of St John's looking towards the altar. At the far end of the church, not visible, are a number of military flags standing in the corners.

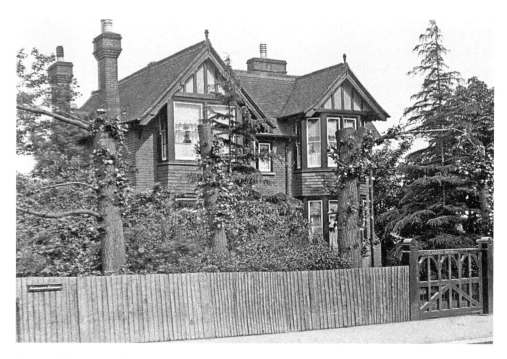

Clarence House was a five-bedroom house close to the station, which, when it was sold, was listed as situated in the best part of the forest.

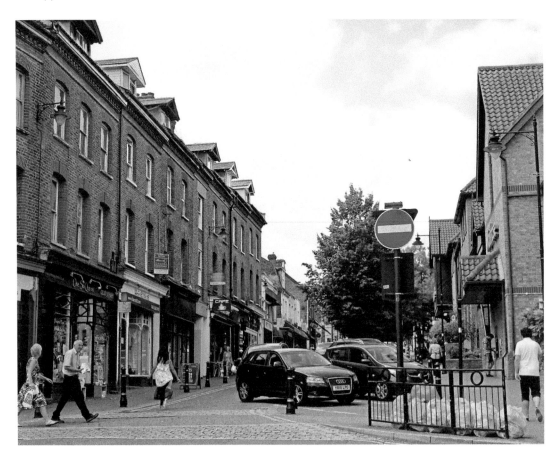

Queen's Road in Buckhurst Hill has retained much of its old charm.

While its resident he employed the famous gardener Humphrey Repton to landscape the grounds. These consisted of 4 to 5 acres in the middle of the forest. It took a lot of work as there was an enormous rabbit warren, which meant a lot of damage to the garden.

In 1863 the *London Illustrated News* reported on the opening of the new National School for 200 children in Staples Road. According to the report Loughton was a pleasant village in the heart of Epping Forest and the school was needed due to the growing population. The building included a residence for the teachers and was paid for by the Revd John Whittaker Maitland and local residents.

There was a different use for the school building in 1881 during an epidemic of Scarlet Fever in the village. The school became a hospital and beds were transferred from the London Hospital at Whitechapel. Doctors also attended the sick children. Most of the children survived the illness, although others had previously died from it. Once the cases were clear the school was cleaned and returned to its normal function.

The school building was later sold to the Shaftsbury Society, who renamed it Ashley Camp House, as a holiday home for children, some of whom were disabled.

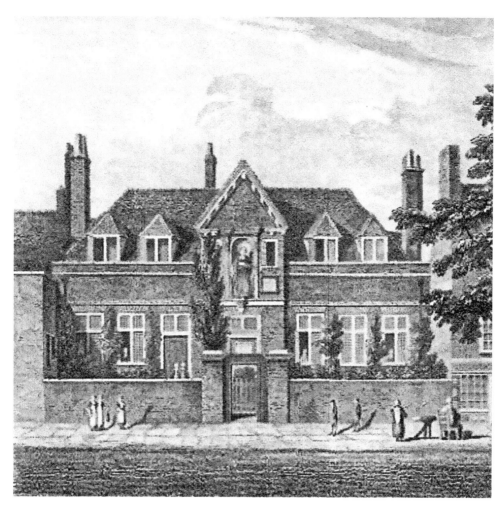

The money used to pay for the National School was raised by local dignitaries.

In 1937 the building was sold and the land used for private housing. It is now known as Ashley Grove.

The Melbourne Retreat was a house that was used to sell refreshments to visitors to Loughton until the late nineteenth century. It was then purchased by the Ragged School Union, a charity that took children from London on day trips to the country. It was renamed the Shaftesbury Retreat. Retreats were a common venue in the majority of villages and hamlets between Woodford and Epping. They catered for the many visitors to the forest.

The Melbourne Retreat was taken over by the council in 1939 when the Second World War broke out and was converted into a mortuary for air-raid victims. After the war it was used for some time as a glassworks. In 1968 housing was built in the area but the superintendent's house has survived as well as the name Shaftesbury in the road that runs through the grounds.

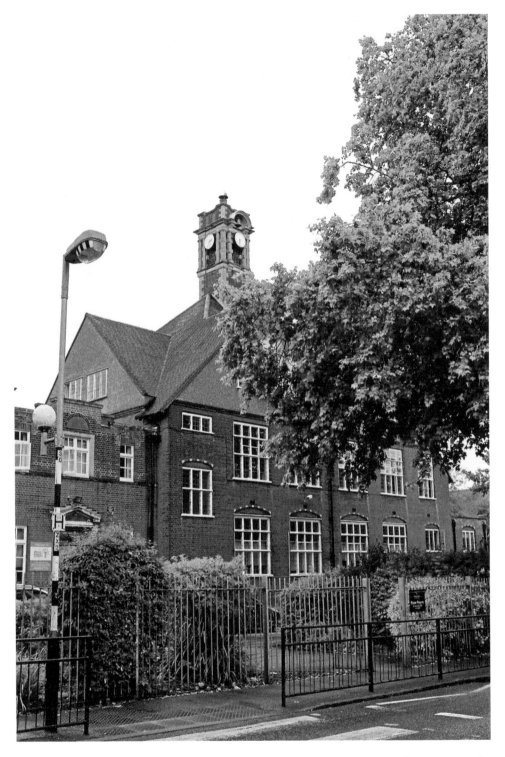

Roding Valley High School opened in 1908. Winifred Darch, the children's author, was once the headmistress.

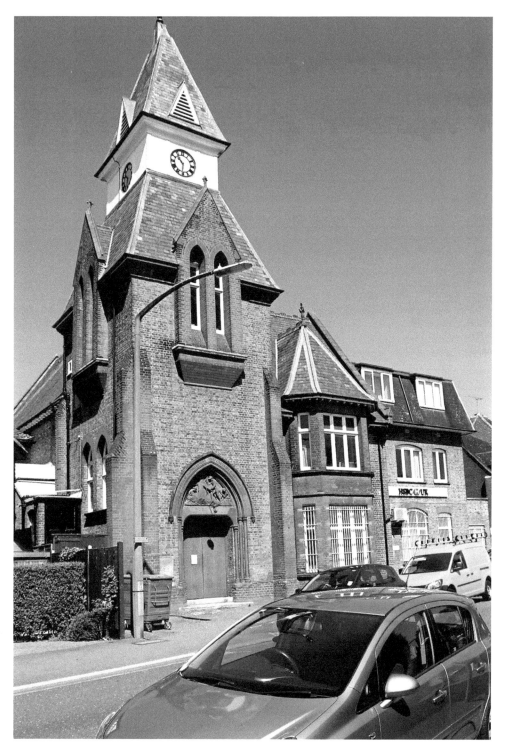

Lopping Hall was built with money from the sale of the forest to the Corporation of London for the benefit of the local people.

3. Shops and Businesses

DID YOU KNOW THAT ?

At the end of the nineteenth century two shops in Loughton were selling a form of baby powder that was responsible for the deaths of thirteen children and the non-fatal injuries of sixteen other infants.

The events led to the trial at the Old Bailey of the chemist who made the powder. The events were so well publicised in the press that it alerted mothers and shopkeepers in other parts of the country to the danger of the powder.

One industry that could have caused a great deal of damage to the forest was shipbuilding, and it nearly happened in the forest area surrounding Loughton as in 1663 the diarist Samuel Pepys, a naval man, tried to speed up the transport of timber from the forest for shipbuilding. The trees that were felled were taken to Barking and floated in the creek to the shipyards of the Thames. The use of trees from Epping Forest for shipbuilding went on until 1725.

Pepys had other associations with Loughton, as he was a friend of Sir John Mennes, who lived at the Meads. Despite this reported friendship, it seems that Pepys was not happy at Sir John being named Comptroller of the Admiralty – for, according to Pepys, he did nothing but harm.

The obvious early industry in Loughton was farming, and there were also flour mills and some windmills in the area dating back to the eighteenth century. Another industry that grew in Loughton was brick-making. The demand for bricks had grown as a result of increasing housing development.

The soil in Epping Forest was ideal for brick-making and there were several brick- and tile-making works in the Loughton area. There are names that commemorate this such as Claypit Hill at High Beech and Brickyard Cottages near Epping, but more physical evidence can be seen in the hollows that exist in the forest where this industry took place. Brick-making continued well into the twentieth century.

An event in November 1872 was to put Loughton amongst the leading areas for mechanised farming. William Smith was a leading proponent of the steam plough. Although he didn't come from the area, in November he used his plough in Loughton fields, an event important enough to be reported in *The Times*. Smith claimed to have carried out the ploughing for six shillings and four pence halfpenny an acre. His mechanisation of farming was to increase farm production throughout the nineteenth century.

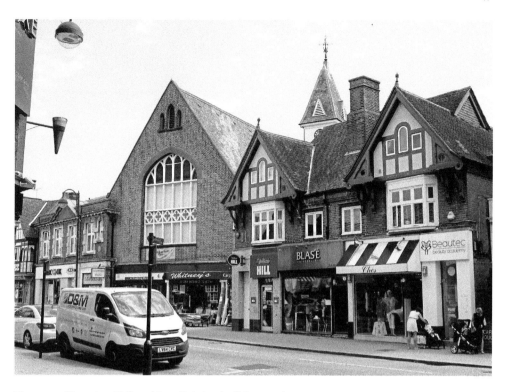

The rear of Lopping Hall and its adjoining buildings today.

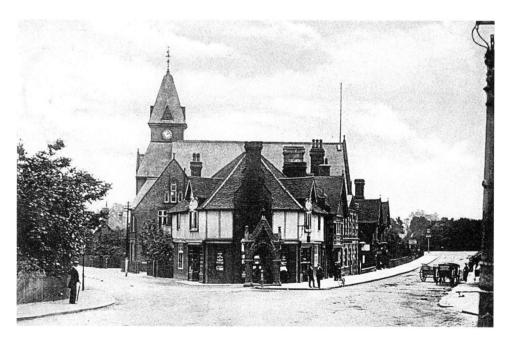

An old view of the High Road showing the original ornate fountain that was destroyed in a road accident.

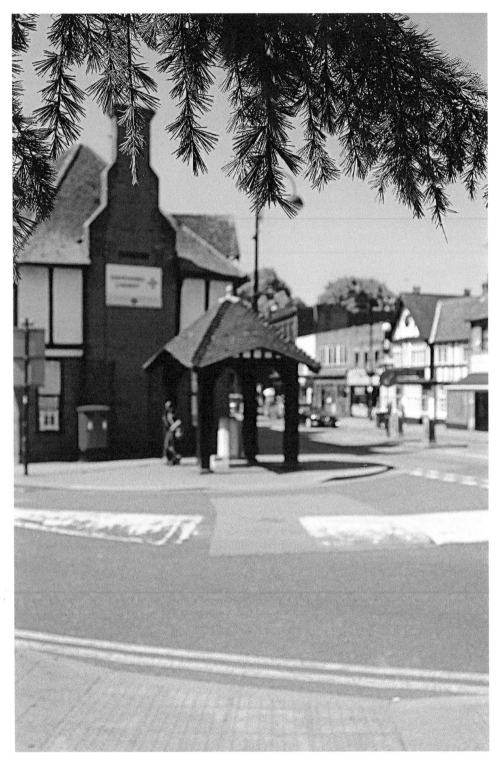

The old fountain has been replaced by a much more basic one.

The owner of one of the shops in Loughton in 1883 found himself in enough trouble to be reported in the national press. Thomas Warriner, a provision dealer of High Road, was convicted of having a fraudulent weighing machine in his shop. It was a quarter of an ounce against the purchaser, which may not seem much but if you were buying goods on a regular basis from the shop it would mount up.

Some of the few shops left in the High Street in the nineteenth century sold a type of powder for use in the nursery. It was known as Violet Powder and it had a great influence on the population. Two grocer's shops, at Baldwin's Hill and in the High Street, sold the powder, although it seems that they were unaware of the dangerous content of what they were selling.

Between October 1877 and March 1878 there were thirteen infant deaths in the area as well as sixteen other non-fatal illnesses in young infants due to skin disease or poisoning. This attracted the attention of the Medical Officer of Health in 1878. At the Epping Petty Sessions May 1878 Henry George King, wholesale chemist of Kingsland Road, London, was charged with the unlawful killing of Elizabeth Sears in February 1877. He was charged with unlawfully and fraudulently selling Violet Powders with arsenic, which was used on the bodies of those of tender years and endangered their health. It was claimed that the powder contained between 28 and 51 per cent arsenic, which was cheaper than the starch the powder also contained. King was told to stop selling the powder by the Treasury but did not reply until visited by Sergeant Roots from Scotland Yard.

John Nottage, a grocer from Loughton, had bought a gross of the powders from King for one shilling and nine pence and had thought that it was the purest of powders

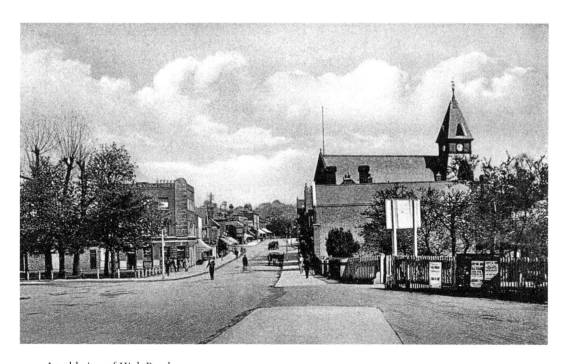

An old view of High Road.

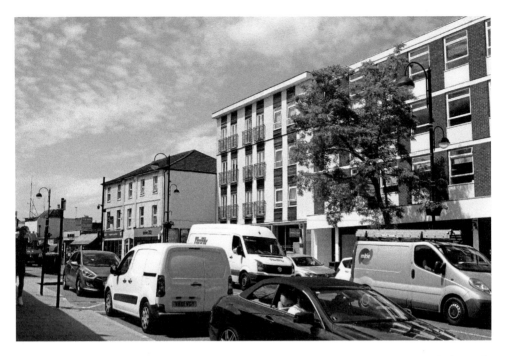

A modern view of the High Road showing how newer buildings have now appeared alongside older ones.

for use in the nursery. Nottage sold the powders for one penny a packet; he had sold powders from other sources in the past with no complaints. When a Mr Deacon complained about the powder he stopped selling it and contacted Mr King. He asked for a warranty as to the powder's safety and King took some of the packets for testing. Nottage heard no more until someone from the Treasury arrived and took all the rest of the powders.

Emma Grout, a grocer of Baldwin's Hill, Loughton, had known King for some years; she bought three dozen packets of the powder from him. Mr Bull, the inspector of nuisances, called on Mrs Grout after complaints from Mrs Martin, Mrs Scars and Mrs Mead. She wrote to King, who again took some of the packets for testing.

Sarah Mead, of Benjamin's Mead, Loughton, had a child in January 1877 named William. She had bought the Violet Powder at Grout's shop, which had King's name and address on it. She used it until March with no ill effects. She then purchased some more, which made the child very red and sore where used. This then turned into blisters. She called Doctor Fowler and stopped using the powder, and the child got better. She then gave the remaining powder to Mr Bell.

Isabella Martin, of Ash Green, Loughton, had a baby on 21 November 1877. She bought some Violet Powder from Grout's shop and after using it for nine days the baby died. Where she had applied the powder there were a number of black blisters. Again Mr Bell took the powder away. Hannah Reid, also of Ash Green, had been Mrs Martin's midwife and said that the baby had been healthy when born.

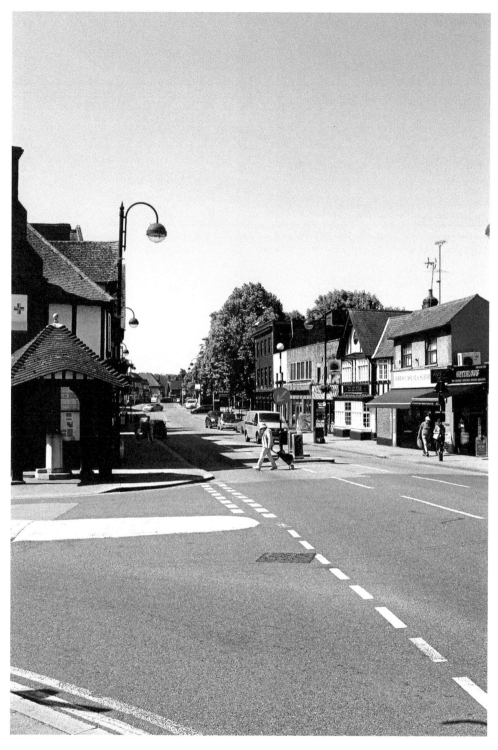

The High Road showing the fountain on the left and some of the mixture of old and new buildings that now line the road.

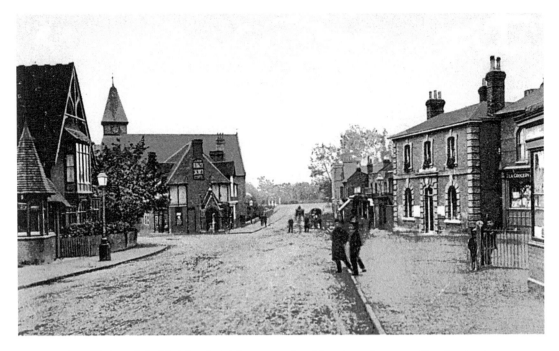

Another old view of the High Road with houses on the right where shops now line the street.

Elizabeth Sears of Baldwin's Hill, Loughton, had one child early in 1877. She used King's powder from Grout's and the baby died after a week. She had another baby in February 1878 and bought more of the powder, and the second child died at a week old. The baby had been healthy at birth but had died in agony.

King said that he was well known in Loughton and that his mother-in-law lived next door to one of the witnesses. He very much regretted that the powder may have been the cause of the deaths and said that he would have stopped selling it if he had known. The case was adjourned on a number of occasions and during the various hearings expert witnesses were called.

It seemed that arsenic was sold for ten shillings a ton, which was much cheaper than the starch normally used in the powders. Doctor Du Pre from Westminster Hospital also examined the powders and found that some contained up to 51 per cent arsenic. It was also said that it was very easy to see the difference between arsenic and the normal starch used in the powder. It was also evident from press reports that the adulterated Violet Powder was on sale all over London, not just in Loughton. Some of this was due to King but not all. There were also cases of adulterated powder being sold in Manchester, where two chemists were fined, but in this case it was sulphate of lime not arsenic that was used.

King claimed during the trial that he bought the powder to make the Violet Powders from other chemists and that once he knew that they may be dangerous he tried to stop the sale of them. The trial was moved from Epping Assizes to Essex Assizes and eventually to the Old Bailey. King was released on bail for £200. The trial eventually ended with King being found not guilty as it was found that the inclusion of arsenic in the powder was accidental.

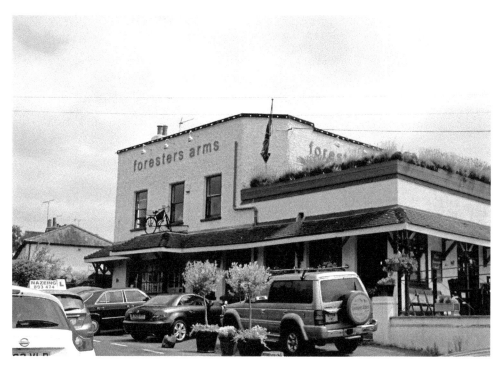

The Forresters Arms is on Baldwin's Hill, facing towards the forest. One must wonder how many famous customers have visited the pub in the past with there being so many well-known neighbours.

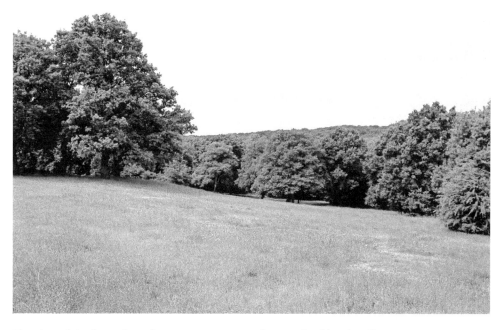

The view of the forest from the Forresters Arms at the top of Baldwin's Hill.

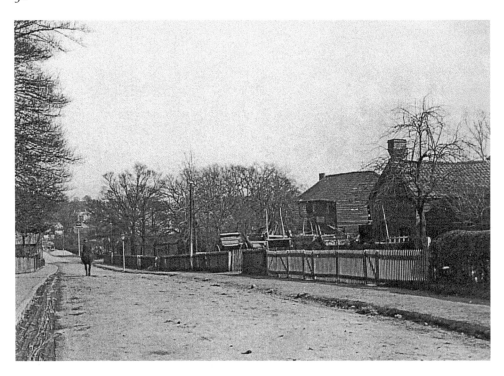

An old view of Church Hill, which runs between the High Road and Goldings Hill.

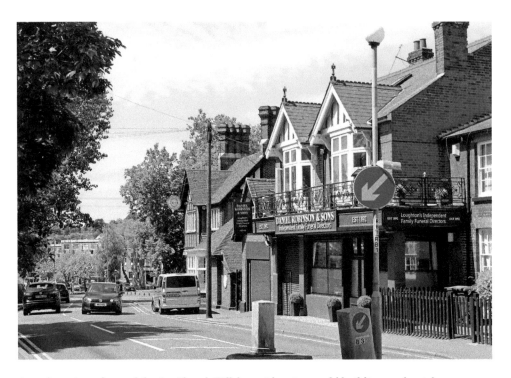

A modern view of a much busier Church Hill, but with quite an old building on the right.

4. Crime

DID YOU KNOW THAT ?

Dick Turpin once ran a butcher's shop in Loughton. Many of the tales associated with Turpin came from later works of fiction which portrayed him as a gentleman, but he was in fact a vicious thug.

Turpin and his gang committed a number of robberies in the Loughton area. Many of these were as highwaymen, holding up stagecoaches or travellers on their way through the forest. Turpin's gang also robbed homes and were not adverse to using torture to get what they wanted – in one case supposedly roasting an old lady over her own fire to find out where she had hidden her money.

Local residents had no illusions about Turpin; many added 'Turpin traps' to their homes. This was a wooden flap that was lowered over the stairs and held in place with a pole braced against the ceiling, which stopped anyone getting upstairs.

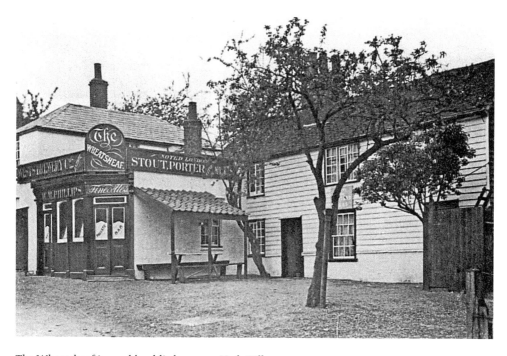

The Wheatsheaf is an old public house on York Hill.

One of the problems in the Loughton area when it came to crime was the presence of deer. The fact that these animals were present in the forest was a great temptation to those who had little to eat. In 1807 Arthur Young wrote a report for the Great British Board of Agriculture which said that the 'forests of Epping and Hainault are viewed as a terrible nuisance. They are known to be the nursery and resort of the most idle and profligate men, the undergraduates in iniquity commence their career with deer stealing and here the more hardened robbers secrete themselves from justice'.

The most famous criminal connected to Loughton is of course Dick Turpin, who was born near Saffron Walden but spent some time in the Loughton area. There are a number of crimes attributed to Turpin, many of which have a basis in fiction such as his famous ride to York, which may have occurred but was actually carried out by another highwayman named William Nevison. Many of the rumours about Turpin can be traced back to a novel called *Rookwood* published in 1824 by Harrison Ainsworth, including the ride to York.

In his early twenties Turpin had a butcher's shop at Buckhurst Hill, and from here he began to sell stolen deer meat. He was probably responsible for stealing sheep too. It was after being found out that he progressed to more serious crime. It is believed that after leaving his business he became involved in smuggling on the Essex coast. He is also believed to have passed himself off as a revenue officer and to have robbed the smugglers of their goods. This obviously did not make him popular, and he then returned to the Epping area.

Turpin then joined a gang who were responsible for stealing deer. The gang may have been the same men who had previously supplied him with stolen meat for his shop. They

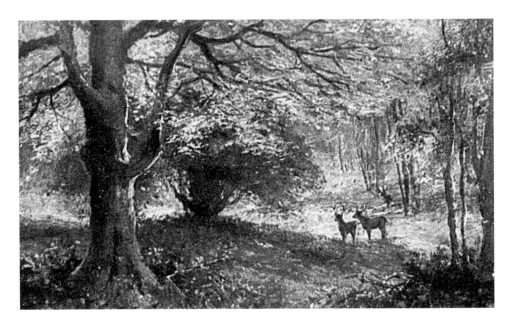

An animal that has played an important part in the history of the forest is the deer – used for hunting by royalty in the distant past and stolen by criminals in the more recent past.

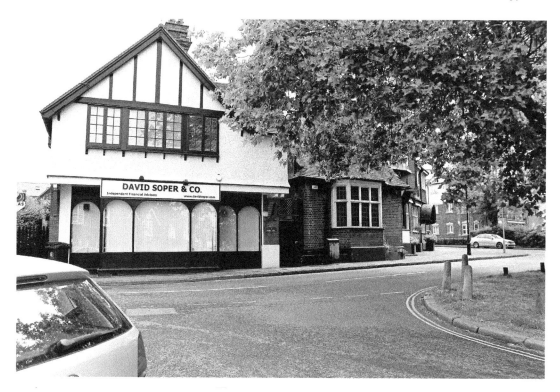

Pump Hill is shown at the junction with Church Lane, next to the war memorial and what was The Crown public house.

were known as the Gregory Gang and they lived in London but often committed robberies in the Epping area. These robberies included stealing from churches. In 1735 they robbed an elderly lady in Loughton and supposedly roasted her over her own fire to find out where her money was hidden. They were no strangers to violence.

The gang were eventually caught, although Turpin escaped. A number of the gang were hanged, so Turpin then began to work alone or with one other highwayman. Turpin left the area for a few years, robbing around London. One story claims that he attempted to rob a man who turned out to be Tom King, another well-known highwayman, which led to their joining forces.

Turpin obviously returned to his roots as there were reports in some of the newspapers of the time, such as the *Country Journal* of 24 May 1737, who stated that the previous day Turpin had robbed two coaches in Epping Forest. In the *London Gazette* of 7 June 1737 it stated that the Saffron Walden and Bishop Stortford coaches were stopped near Epping Forest and despite their being up to twenty passengers, he still robbed them and made off with their possessions.

The pair were traced after stealing a man's horse at Leytonstone because the horse was a well-known steeplechaser and was recognised in a stable at Whitechapel. While trying to capture the pair King was accidentally shot and blamed Turpin. There is some discrepancy as to whether the shot was fatal or not, but Turpin fled to Epping Forest,

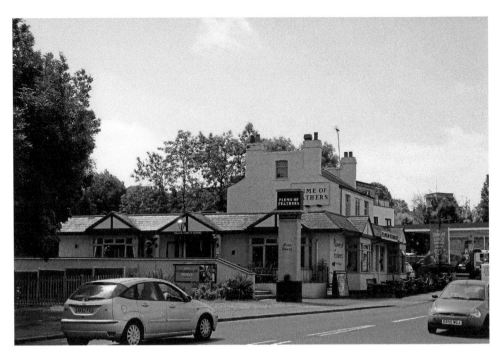

Another old Loughton public house, the Plume of feathers, which stands at the Goldings Hill end of Church Hill.

A view from Pump Hill that shows the wonderful range of countryside visible from the hills of Loughton.

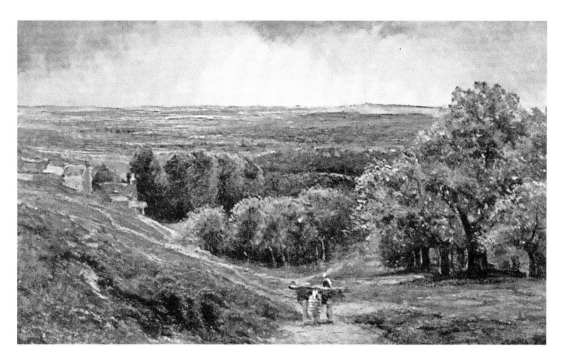

An old postcard with a view towards what was known as Dick Turpin's Cave. This is where he supposedly hid from pursuit.

where he was supposedly found hiding in what was described as a cave. There is some dispute over whether this took place in Epping Forest, but there is a place known as Turpin's Cave near High Beech. This was more likely to have been a hollow in one of the walls of Loughton Camp.

When he was found he shot one of the forest keepers. He then left Essex and moved north, where he began life as a horse dealer. There are conflicting reports of Turpin, now known as John Palmer, who either shot or stole a valuable game cock used for fighting. After being arrested it was discovered that he was really Dick Turpin. He was later charged with horse theft and was hanged at York Castle in 1739.

It seems that Turpin was not the only highwayman operating in the Loughton area during the eighteenth century. The roads were patrolled by cavalry every night to combat gangs of ruffians known as the Waltham Blacks. Many of the members of these gangs were ex-soldiers who had fought in the Civil War and had no employment after it ended.

One of these gangs once almost captured William III on his way through the forest to Newmarket. The gang were camped in the Wake Valley. One traveller who took shelter in an inn for the night saw a ceremony at the inn involving highwaymen and their king, Oronoco. Although these gangs may have been responsible for deer stealing, many of the locals were not averse to doing the same.

Claims of sheep stealing may have generally been limited to the odd animal, such as those that ended up in Dick Turpin's shop, but in 1843 there was a theft on a much bigger

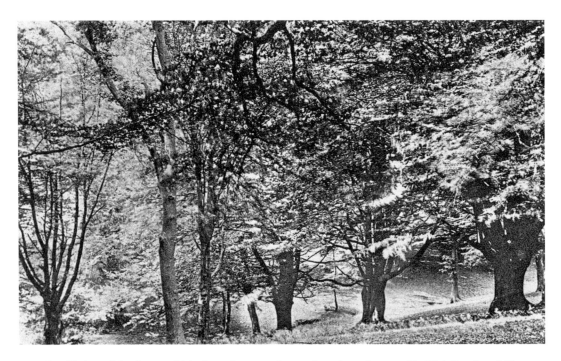

An old view of the forest, which shows how easy it must have been for men like Dick Turpin to hide from anyone pursuing them.

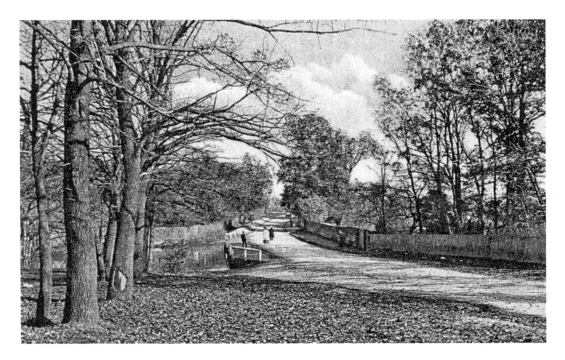

It wasn't only the trees that attracted people to the forest but the numerous ponds. They were at times said to be abused by visitors swimming in them.

scale. Charles Croucher was a master drover who lived in Loughton with his three sons. They found themselves incarcerated at Ilford House of Correction, and from here they were taken to the Waltham Abbey Sessions in May. They were charged with stealing 123 sheep from Mr James Wickham of Wonston in Hampshire.

Mr Wickham's shepherd had counted his sheep in the previous November and found that he had 1,423. In January, after noticing a certain sheep was missing, he recounted and found only 1,300. Croucher had been seen driving a flock of more than 100 sheep, which he claimed he had bought from someone called Mr Stubbs, but the sheep had been branded JW. Several of these sheep were found in the possession of various people, including Revd Archdeacon Hamilton of Loughton. All the new owners stated that they bought them from Croucher.

Mr Wickham's shepherd claimed to recognise the sheep as those belonging to his master. He claimed to be able to recognise all of Mr Wickham's sheep, despite there being more than a 1,000 of them.

Theft in Loughton did not always involve armed robbery or even sheep stealing. In a debtors court there were claims of fraud and breach of trust against widow Mary Nash of Buckhurst Hill against a man who had been a practitioner of law, a corn dealer, a carcass butcher, a grocer, a lighterman and, in the case in question, a Methodist parson. It was in this occupation that the defendant had befriended the widow of a professional man and left her destitute. Strangely the man was not named in the report.

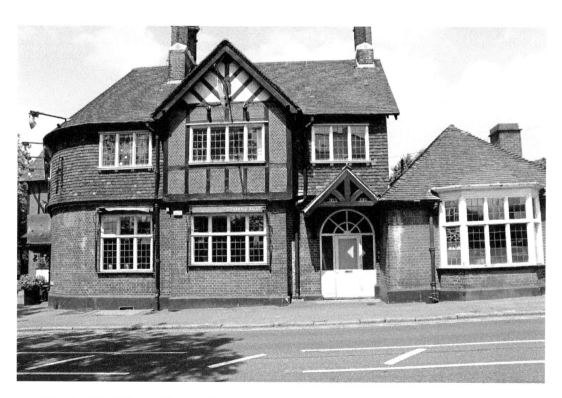

A lovely old building on Church Hill, near to the war memorial.

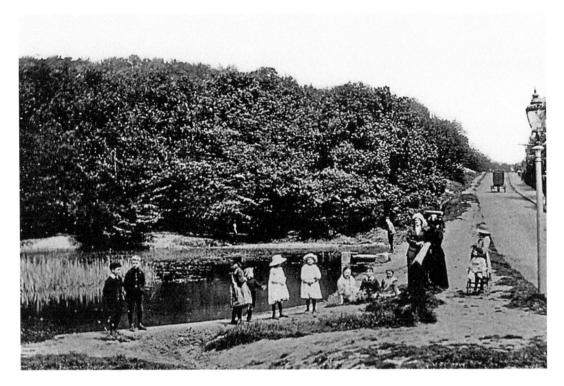

This pond has attracted some young visitors.

The lady's husband had died without providing for her and her husband's brother had given her an annual sum to keep her. She had managed to save some money from this allowance in case her brother-in-law should not be able to continue to support her. She was visited by the defendant, who would read religious texts to her and pray with her.

The defendant claimed to have the lease of an estate at Sewardstone near Waltham Cross, but this was reliant on his performing some duties. He offered to sell this lease to the lady, who had saved £90 and which would give her a sum of £14 a year for life. He drew up an agreement, which, as it turned out, was worthless. He had no intention of carrying out the liabilities, which made the lease void. The defendant was remanded for gross fraud.

In November 1849 a tragic accident led to the death of a young woman. An inquest was held in Loughton into the death of Elizabeth Hughes, aged twenty-three, who had been shot at the house of Mr Thomas, a feather merchant of London who also had a house in Loughton where Hughes was a servant.

Mr Thomas had come down from London and at around eleven o'clock in the morning he had taken a gun from where it was hanging in the kitchen, planning to go and shoot small birds. He was told by a servant that the gun was not loaded. The servant gave Mr Thomas a percussion cap, which he put in the gun just as Hughes walked into the kitchen. The gun went off and the young woman was shot. The woman

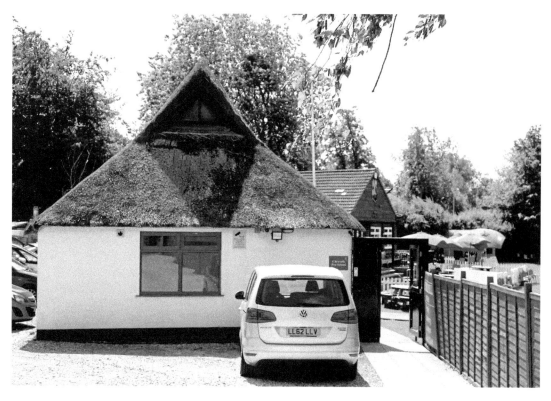

The entrance to the cricket club is in The Uplands, but it is situated on Church Hill.

died before the doctor arrived. Those present all claimed that they did not know the gun was loaded or how it came to be fired. The jury returned a verdict of 'Excusable Homicide'.

It seems that gentlemen in the nineteenth century did not always behave as such. At the Guildhall in June a case of assault was heard involving a girl of sixteen against a resident of Loughton described as a gentleman of fortune and a captain in the army. He was not, however, named in the report.

The girl, who had been living with the gentleman, went into the house of a laundress, Mrs Hutt, in great distress. She had been dragged about by her hair and had wounds as if she had been kicked in the face and body; many of her teeth were loose. She also had several stripes on her body as if she had been whipped. She had to stay in bed for a fortnight due to her injuries.

The gentleman claimed that the girl had been unfaithful to him and expressed the intention to 'do for her yet'. The jury found for the girl and damages of £100 were awarded. The report also went on to say that due to it being Derby Day an unusually high number of jurors applied to be excused from serving due to old age infirmity or illness.

In April 1867 there was an attempted murder by a young man, Frederick Watkins. He had for two years been walking out with a young woman, Matilda Gripps, the daughter of a well sinker of Princess Road, Buckhurst Hill. He had accused her of speaking to other

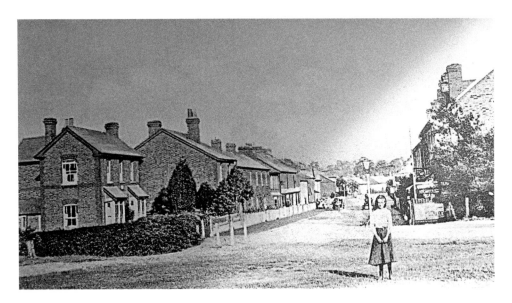

The view is from an old postcard that says Loughton Forest Vale, but there does not seem to be a Forest Vale in the town.

young men and had stabbed her thirteen times. A policeman found her leaning against a fence in a field, covered in blood.

Watkins gave himself up at Epping police station. He admitted trying to kill her and said that he had tried to poison himself after the attack by swallowing oxalic acid but as it was in powder form it only burnt his mouth. He said he did not go to Loughton police station because he thought they may be asleep, and arrived at Epping in the middle of the night.

Watkins said that he had been seeing the girl for two years and she had had his child. He had been giving her money ever since the child was born. The child was four months old when he had begun to get very jealous of her and had also quarrelled with his family over her. While in court he was allowed to cross the room and kiss her.

The Times of 20 July 1876 printed a letter from a church member of St Augustine's, Stepney. According to the letter children from the church along with children from two schools went on a trip to Loughton accompanied by police officers. As was the norm, the children were allowed to make their own way through the forest.

On returning home the children recounted to their mothers how when they had sat down to eat dinner they were approached by a group of men and women who rushed out of the woods and stole their jackets. One of the men also went through the children's pockets looking for money. The children described the robbers as gypsies who also threatened to cut their throats if they told anyone and produced knives to threaten them with.

There was a murder in Loughton in the summer of 1878, when Charles Revell killed his wife by cutting her throat. Revell was at once suspected of the murder due to the threats he had issued towards his wife in the past. The couple were poor and the murder

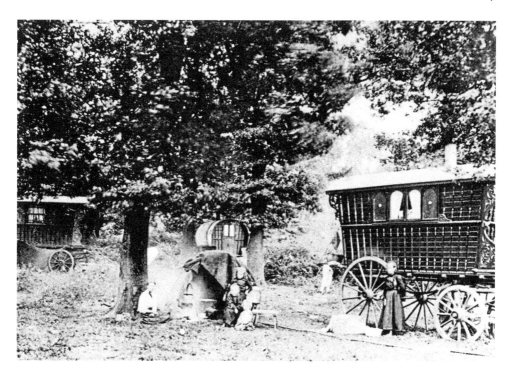

Gypsy camps were common in the forest and there were times when they were blamed for crime in the area.

was a result of the wife trying to stop her husband spending the three shillings he had stolen from her. There was an interesting development during the trial. Revell could not afford to employ a solicitor, but some local people who opposed the death penalty paid for him to be represented by a solicitor from Romford. The fact that he was represented led Revell to believe he would be acquitted. The evidence was too strong, however, and he was hanged at Chelmsford Prison.

The worthy local people of Loughton often had problems with their staff but there was an unusual event in August 1881 at the home of the Revd A. Leeman of Stirling Lodge. Mrs Leeman had observed her cook Louisa Bass acting strangely, as though ill for a week. She then found the cook burning something in the stove and accused her of having a baby.

The cook took Mrs Leeman to her bedroom and pointed to a box. In the box Mrs Leeman found the body of a baby with a string tied around its neck. Bass claimed that the father had promised to marry her, which he later confirmed. In court a surgeon suggested that he could not confirm whether the child had been alive when it was born. The jury returned an open verdict.

Jealousy was, it seems, the cause of another tragedy in the area. In June 1884 a young woman aged nineteen years committed suicide because she believed that her young man was seeing other girls. Jane Gibbings of Nile Cottages, High Beech Road, left a note for her mother saying that she had been visited by the Devil, who had said that her young man

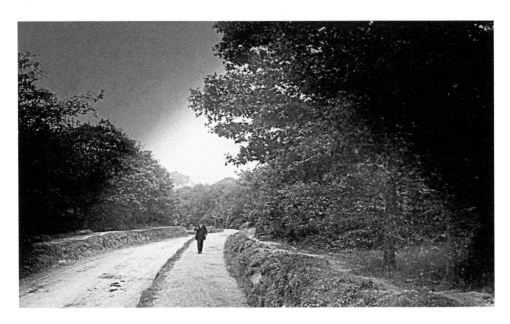

An old view of Earl's Path leading from Loughton up to High Beech.

was seeing other women. The Devil then told her to jump in the water butt and he would send the man to get her out. The girl's mother said that her daughter had been acting very strangely since having an argument with the boy.

The exploitation of visitors to the forest did not only involve robbing them and threatening them with violence. In September 1887 George Hatson, a painter, of Forest Road, Loughton, was charged at Stratford of feloniously demanding and obtaining ten shillings by menace.

Ernest Edward Carpenter had visited Loughton with a lady. They sat on a seat near the keeper's cottage. Hatson approached the couple and claimed to be an official of the forest. He told them that they had no business there and that he had seen them acting in an indecent manner. Carpenter denied this but offered Hatson two shillings, hoping it would get rid of him. Hatson refused the money but said that unless he was given ten shillings he would go to the law.

Carpenter paid him the ten shillings but later went to the forest keeper to complain. They went looking for Hatson but could not find him. Carpenter returned to Loughton a few days later and saw him. Hatson was then arrested. The court, however, discharged Hatson. They said that they were suspicious of him but that there was insufficient evidence.

The increase of visitors to the forest was another factor influencing the rise in crime. Although many people came to the forest by train, there was another form of transport that was becoming very popular in the late nineteenth century: the bicycle. Those interested in cycling were appearing in all areas and it wasn't unusual to see large groups of cyclists on the roads.

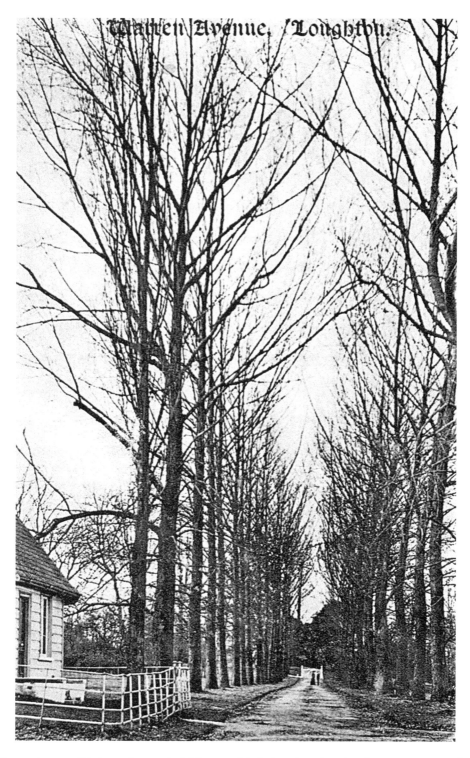

Warren Avenue: this is another card which states it is in Loughton but that does not seem to exist. I suspect it was once known by this name but may have been built on since and the name changed.

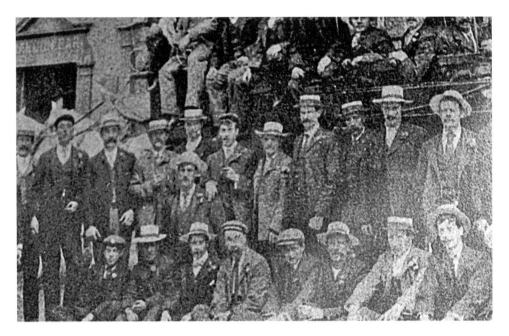

A group of men about to go on a day out to the forest. The men are probably workers from a factory.

In August 1887 a Loughton man appeared in court at Stratford charged with an offence that had taken place in June. James Edwards of Beech Hill Park was a Justice of the Peace for Essex on the Epping bench. He was charged with assaulting Ernest James Evans, the secretary of the Upton Park Bicycling Club.

Evans claimed that he and five companions had been cycling from Waltham Abbey towards Stratford at around 9 p.m. in the evening. They all had their lamps burning. As they approached the New Inn Edwards came towards them driving a pair horse wagonette. Edwards was in the centre of the roadway and as they passed he struck at one of the cyclists, Mr Mattada, with his whip and then struck Evans across the face, drawing blood. He then drove off at a rapid pace saying, 'That will teach you to keep to your right side.'

Edwards said that he was driving two guests to the station when he was confronted by the cyclists, who, according to one witness, appeared to be all over the place like a swarm of bees. Edwards called on them to keep to their side but two of them cut across in front of the horses. He admitted flicking at them with his whip but not in a vicious manner. He denied saying what Evans said he did and driving off rapidly.

Evans claimed that three of the cyclists passed Edwards on the right side of the road to avoid a pile of stones on the other side. The other three crossed over in front of the horses to pass him on the other side. The bench said that they found that an assault had been committed without justification but that there had been some provocation. They imposed only a nominal fine of five shillings.

A month after the cycling court case there was a further traffic-related incident when Samuel Oliver, a carman for a mineral water company, was driving down Buckhurst Hill with a van and pair of horses. He ran over Frederick Smith, aged seventy- seven, and killed

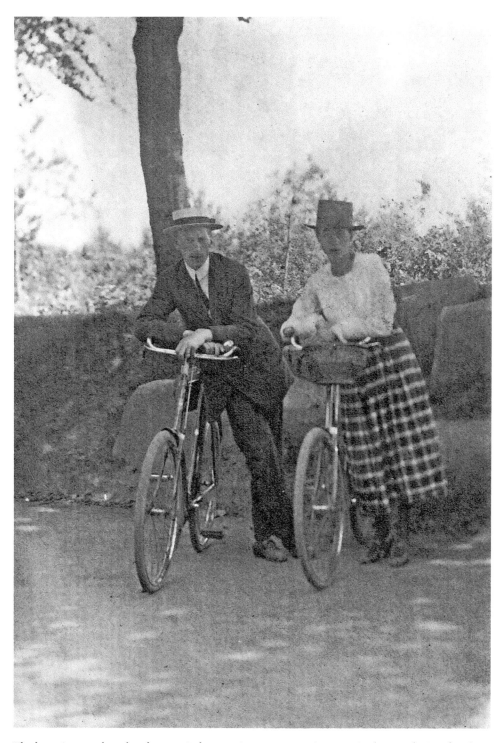

The late nineteenth and early twentieth centuries saw a great increase in the popularity of cycling. Even those of the lower classes could often afford this cheap means of travel, which meant they could reach the forest from distant parts of London.

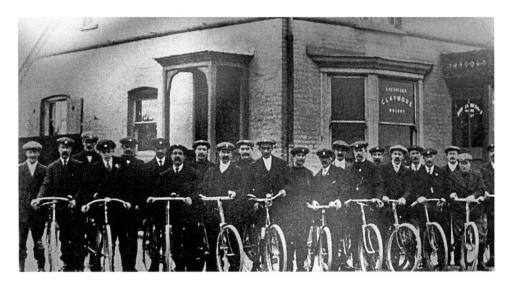

Cycling clubs often had large numbers of members who would go out together on trips to places such as Epping Forest. This led at times to conflict with those using other forms of transport.

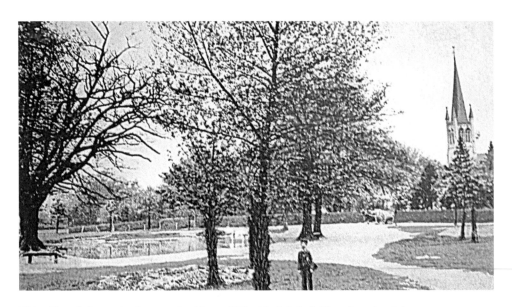

This old card shows the Green at Buckhurst Hill with St John's Church to the right.

him. Oliver was found to have been negligent and was found guilty of manslaughter and given six months' hard labour.

In April 1893 a Loughton labourer, George Luffman of Ash Green, found himself in Stratford Court charged with unlawfully and maliciously setting fire to a quantity of heather near Dulsmead Hollow. The heather was described as belonging to the Corporation of the City of London.

At 10 p.m. on a Sunday night one of the forest keepers saw Luffman deliberately strike three matches and throw them on the heather. When he saw the keeper he tried to trample on it. When accused of lighting the fire he denied it, claiming he had been lighting his pipe. Mr McKenzie, the superintendent of the forest, said that there had been ten or twelve fires lately and Luffman was seen coming away from one of them. He was described as a notorious character who had been under observation for two years. He was remanded, but unfortunately the outcome of the trial is unknown.

The perception of the Victorian period in regards to the treatment of children is a poor one, with the exploitation of children in factories and harsh treatment in workhouses. It is a surprise then to find that a child living in Buckhurst Hill in 1897 was the subject in a court case brought by the National Society of the Prevention of Cruelty to Children, which had been founded in 1884. It was claimed that the child's parents, of Hope Villas, King's Place, Buckhurst Hill, had mistreated their child over a period of eighteen months, which eventually led to its death aged two and a half years. The couple had two older children and two younger who were well-treated. The child was regularly heard screaming by the couple's neighbours. When examined the child had a fracture of the right leg and right forearm and died soon after from what the doctor claimed was malnutrition.

The child's grandfather claimed that the child had been delicate from birth and that the mother had been in a weak state at the birth due to a fall. A witness who had seen the

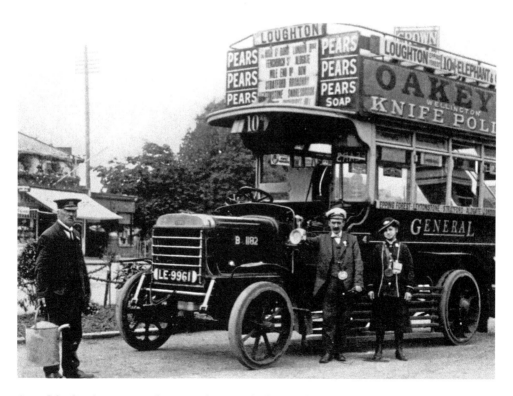

One of the first buses to run from Loughton to Elephant and Castle, London.

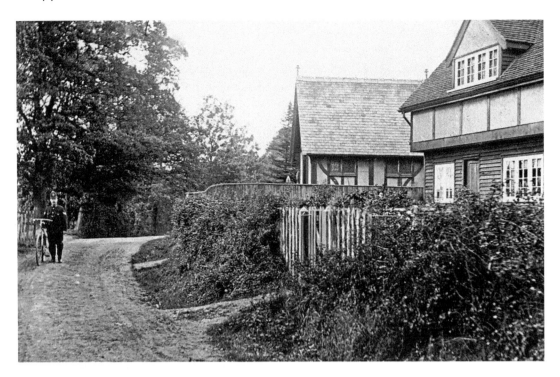

There were fewer policemen in Loughton in the past. In one case a man wishing to admit to an attempted murder went to Epping police station, in case they were all asleep in Loughton.

child was told that the doctor had said there was nothing wrong with it, but it seemed that the child was not under a doctor at the time of its death. The parents were committed to trial.

As time progressed it was no longer horse-drawn vehicles that were a danger to cyclists but motor vehicles. In July 1908 it was once again a dignitary who was involved in an accident with cyclists. Driver James Morris found himself in Stratford Court for negligently driving a motorcar and for not giving his name and address. It was not Morris who was the dignitary, however, but his passenger, the Archbishop of Westminster – Morris was his driver.

A witness said that in late June he had been cycling along Epping New Road towards Loughton and saw two young ladies cycling in front of him on the right side of the road. As the Archbishop's car overtook them the mudguard caught one of the cycles, causing both of them to fall. The car stopped along the road but when the witness approached and asked the driver for his name he refused to give it and drove off.

The car was then stopped by the police. One of the ladies' fathers said that the driver offered her two shillings for a damaged spoke and said 'you are not hurt'. He then increased his offer to half a crown. The driver of the car claimed he saw the cyclists, who were wobbling; he had sounded his horn and did not know he had hit one of them. The magistrate decided that there had been no negligence and refusing to give his name was a technical offence, so fined Morris a shilling.

In a quiet area such as Loughton the police in 1930 probably didn't expect to deal with threats from gunmen. However on 11 July police constable Alfred Charles James saw a man in what he believed to be a stolen car. He was not happy with the man's explanation as to how he had obtained the car and threatened to arrest him. The man then produced a pistol, which he thrust against the constable's body, and threatened to shoot him. James then grappled with the man and while a violent struggle was taking place two passers-by came to the policeman's aid. The man was arrested and was also found to be carrying a knife. He was sent to prison for twelve months, which seemed quite lenient considering the offence. Constable James was awarded a £10 cheque for his bravery by the magistrate at Bow Street.

There was a crime involving the military in July 1932 when a private in the Royal Army Service Corps appeared in Stratford Court. James Nicholl was based at Warley Barracks and was charged with causing the deaths of a husband, wife and son of Walthamstow. Nicholl had been driving a War Department Daimler car from London towards Epping when it came into collision with a motorcycle and sidecar.

It seems that guns were quite common in the period between the wars, perhaps due to many men having served in the forces. There was a crime involving a gun that took place in April 1933, although not in Loughton – one of the men involved was a local resident, however.

A Mr Smith of Alderton Hill, Loughton, had, it seemed, shot dead a workmate at a joinery works in Wealdstone and then shot himself. Mr Smith's wife said in court that her

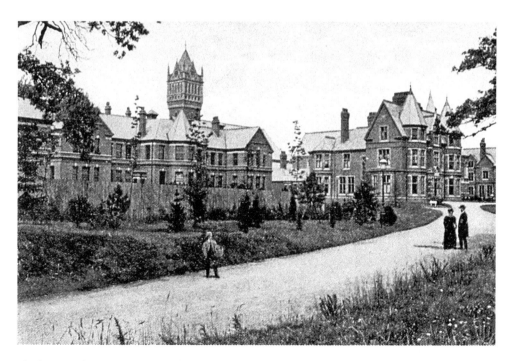

Claybury Asylum wasn't in Loughton but is thought to have been named after a fictional village of the same name. The writer who created it was W. Jacobs.

husband had suffered a number of crashes while serving in the Air Force and it may have been due to this that he suffered from some mental health issues.

Smith worked for the joinery company as a salesman but for the past few years had been acting strangely and had a grudge against a Mr Battye, who he sent abusive letters to. Smith was told that if he wanted to keep his job he had to seek medical advice. The specialist said that he was suffering from delusions but that very few such patients were violent.

It was Mr Battye who pleaded for Smith to be able to keep his job as they had been friends once. Then one morning Smith had entered Mr Battye's office and a clerk heard a shot. Battye came out of his office and said he had been shot. There was another shot, which was Smith shooting himself. Both men died.

An unusual event which took place in September 1934 led to the discovery of a rather unsavoury crime being discovered. The Roman Catholic Church of St Edmund at Traps Hill caught fire and was burned to the ground. The church was a corrugated iron building lined with wood that had been built in 1927. When the ruins of the church were inspected a body was found. The priest in charge of the church said that he had no idea who the body could be but a padlock was found in the dead man's pocket, seeming to show that he had broken in, and the offertory boxes in the church had been rifled.

It was later found that around an hour before the fire broke out a man had entered a café in High Street, Loughton, and was served with bread and tea. The manageress had heard the sound of money being counted and when the man left she found that a Barnardos collection box had been broken open and the money taken.

The dead man was later discovered to be Alfred Noakes of East Dulwich, who had been released from prison in July after serving two years for breaking into a church. He had been in court in August 1932 charged with attempting to steal from an offertory box at St Peter's Church, Westminster. This was within an hour and a half of being released from Pentonville prison, where he had served twelve months for stealing from a church offertory box!

Noakes had thirteen previous convictions: six for attempted larceny or larceny from churches and three for theft of hospital collection boxes from public houses. The magistrate said that persistent thefts from churches seemed to be the man's main occupation. The fire was thought to have started after the man lit a cigarette after he had broken into the church.

It wasn't only crimes committed in the Loughton area that led to work for the local police. In May 1957 there was a widespread manhunt in the area for John Henry Fowler, who had escaped from Dartmoor prison. A police sergeant had reported seeing him at Buckhurst Hill after the sergeant, E. Hardiman, a warrant officer at Epping Court, had reported seeing a man come out of the forest dressed in blue dungarees and a dark blue coat.

The police were aided by forest keepers and police dogs as they searched around Loughton, Buckhurst Hill and High Beech without success. Hardiman claimed he saw the man well and had his picture, and so recognised him instantly. It is a wonder though how a man in prison uniform could have got all the way from Dartmoor to the forest without being seen.

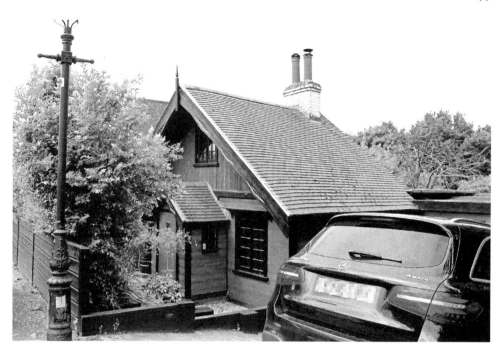

There were a number of keeper's lodges in the forest; this one is on Baldwin's Hill.

In August 1959 Mrs Barbara Mayland of Millsmead Way was returning home with her husband by car at 2 a. m. when a man in Ranger's Road, Epping, signalled them to stop, but they did not do so because they thought he was drunk – they were near a public house.

Later a body was found by the side of the road which showed signs of having been bound and gagged. The body was that of Mr Solomon Lever, a former mayor of Hackney. Mr Lever had been lured from his home after being told that a savings club, of which he was secretary, was threatened by a fire. It was later discovered that nearly £8,000 had been stolen from the club. When shown a photograph of Mr Lever Mrs Mayland said that she recognised him as the man she had seen trying to flag them down.

One of the worst crimes ever committed in Loughton occurred in 1957. A seven-year-old boy, Allen Warren, had been left in his uncle's car outside the Crown Inn on a Saturday evening; his parents and grandparents were inside the pub. Allen came from Lowestoft; he had come to spend a holiday with his grandparents who lived in Smarts Lane, Loughton.

At one point his grandfather had brought an orange juice out to the car and sat with him. It was later found that he was missing. A search began of the local area and Allen's naked body was found on a building site in Connaught Hill by a police constable. He had been murdered.

It was reported that Allen's parents had gone to the Hollybush public house. When they left they saw Allen, who had been at home with his grandmother outside the Standard public house. He said that he wanted to see his uncle. They then went to the Crown Inn

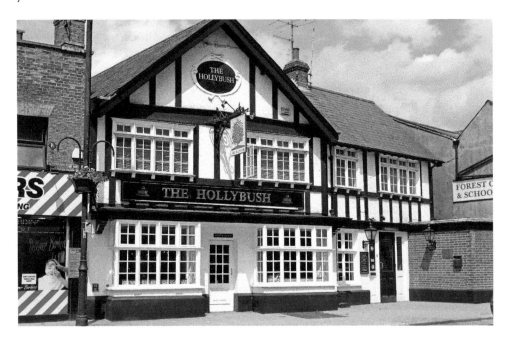

The Hollybush public house in the High Road was a pub where the parents of a murdered boy were drinking on the evening that he disappeared.

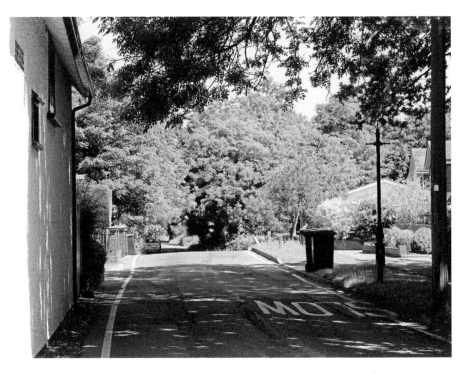

Baldwin's Hill was a popular place for the artistic residents of Loughton, as the number of Blue Plaques in the road show.

and Allen was left in the car. They said that when his grandfather went to collect the empty glass of orange juice Allen had asked for a packet of crisps. When his grandfather came back he was gone.

Allen had been sexually assaulted and suffocated. The police said that they were interviewing patients who were out on parole from Claybury Asyluml on Saturday evening. Other mental hospitals in the area were also visited by the police and other men in the area were interviewed. Some of Allan's missing clothes were later found at Bethnal Green and Leyton railway. Further searches were taking place along the railway lines into London stations.

The boy's uncle, Colin Warren, who also lived in Smarts Lane, appealed for two men named George and Arthur who had accompanied him to some clubs in London to get in touch. Colin was also interviewed on television on BBC's *Tonight* programme. He again asked on television for a man named George, who he had agreed to meet on the night of the murder, to get in touch. A BBC spokesman said after the interview that there had been nothing of this nature on television before. The BBC later apologised for showing the interview, which had not been sanctioned by anyone of a senior position in the corporation.

A man was eventually arrested at Wanstead Hospital and charged with Allen's murder. He was Horace Henry Edwards and had told the police that he didn't mean to kill Allen and wanted to get it off his chest. There was a crowd of around 300 outside Epping Magistrates' Court when Edwards arrived in a police car – many were booing. By the time

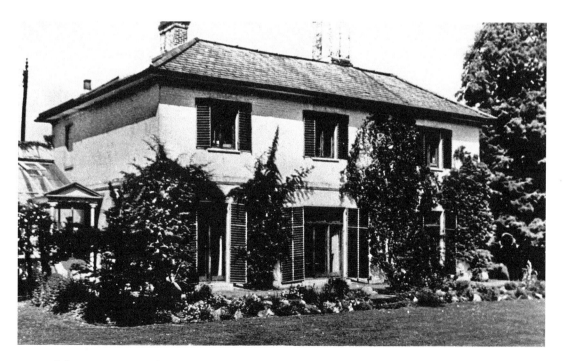

Debden House is part of what was once Debden Hall, which dates back to 1777 and is now a camping and education centre owned by the London Borough of Newham.

he left court the crowd had grown to around 500 and many of them rushed around the back when it was realised that was how he was leaving.

At his trial it was said that Edwards had written a letter to his mother saying that he had been acting strangely lately and that he had killed the boy in Loughton. Edward's sister had found him with his head in the gas oven and the letter on the table.

Despite its gentile image, Loughton was obviously affected by the changes taking place within society in the 1960s. In June 1964 thirty-two youths, eight of them juveniles, were sent for trial at Hertford Assizes from Epping Magistrates' Court. They were charged with the possession of offensive weapons and causing £165 worth of damage to a ballroom. All were granted bail.

The youths were aged between fifteen and nineteen and were mainly from the Loughton and Woodford areas. They were alleged to have caused a disturbance at Ember's Ballroom in Harlow. The prosecution alleged that a raid had been organised as a reprisal after two youths from Debden had been injured in a fight at the ballroom a fortnight earlier.

5. Military

DID YOU KNOW THAT ?

A famous war poet of the First World War lived at High Beech. Edward Thomas was known as a war poet but he actually wrote many poems about Essex while based there as a member of the Artist Rifles Officer Training Corps. While at Romford he spent time training at High Beech. He loved the area so much that he moved his family into an empty cottage there – the owner was at the front fighting. Thomas spent his last leave at the cottage before being killed in France in 1917.

The nineteenth century saw the growth of the Volunteer Rifle Corps in the country. In September 1866 there was a rifle match between a number of these corps, but rather than all coming together they all fired at different ranges. The prize was a silver cup given by Mr Turnham. The three participants were the Finsbury Rifles, the Central London Rifle Rangers and the 6th Tower Hamlets. The completion was to involve twenty men from each unit firing at their own ranges on the same day. The Finsbury Rifles fired at Rainham, the Central London fired at Tottenham Range and the Tower Hamlets at Loughton Range at High Beech.

Epping Forest and Loughton were often involved in training and gatherings of the local militia, which often involved sham battles. In June 1891, 374 men of the 2nd Tower Hamlets Rifles, wearing grey, arrived by train at Loughton station commanded by Lieutenant Colonel Bryan. The 1st Tower Hamlets Rifles, in red and numbering 300, under the command of Colonel Wilde, arrived at Chingford.

The grey force were playing an enemy advancing on London. There were only two roads and a few tracks between them. The grey troops advanced and there was rifle fire between the two groups. The red force were also firing a machine gun. Sham battles such as this between volunteer forces were often seen as enjoyable public spectacles, although how much could be seen in the forest is unclear as there do not seem to be any reports on this event.

The previous battle was re-enacted in part in December the same year when sergeants of the Metropolitan Volunteer Corps met at Loughton station. The object of the exercise was to practise wood fighting from the perspective of an English Brigade retiring on London through the forest before a superior enemy force. The sergeants would be defending a line from Loughton to Sewardstone Green.

The notion of an enemy force approaching London through Epping Forest was a well-practised one. In May 1892 the exercises were repeated with Volunteer Corps again arriving at Loughton by train to prepare defences against the enemy approaching them. Once again it was the Tower Hamlets Rifle Brigade who seemed to have had a close affinity with Loughton.

The corps recruited men from the East End of London, so it would be no surprise if the members were familiar with their training ground in the forest. If they hadn't been there as part of the volunteer force they could well have been there as visitors.

I have read of several such military manoeuvres in the nineteenth century being watched by large numbers of spectators but there had been none mentioned in the previous reports. In October 1894, however, there was a large contingent of volunteers in the forest and a battle did take place. The London Rifle Brigade commanded by Captain Glyn of the Liverpool Regiment arrived at Loughton station. They were playing an invading force looking to find the site for a large camp in the forest which could be held against an attacking force. At Chingford a party of the Honourable Artillery Company Infantry under Captain Birkett and the 2nd West Surrey's cadet battalion under Major Freeman Wills arrived to harass the defenders of the camp.

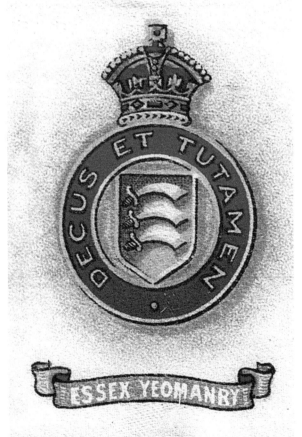

Nº 8. G.P TERRITORIAL BADGES

The Essex Yeomanry badge. Members of the yeomanry would attend weekend and summer camps, where they often took part in sham battles in such places as Epping Forest.

However, the London Rifle Brigade, finding their enemy strung out between Buckhurst Hill and Sewardstone, then became the attacking force. The umpires who were judging the conflict were not mounted and so could not see to stop the companies getting too close to each other and to the reported spectators. Watching sham battles does not seem to have been a very safe pastime, especially in the forest.

The presence of mounted troops in Essex was as common a sight as it was in the rest of the country. The yeomanry had been formed during the Napoleonic Wars as a support for the regular cavalry. They were supposedly only for home defence but did later fight abroad in the Boer War. In 1908 they became part of the territorial force. Loughton had its own unit and along with other Essex squads were often present at local fairs and special occasions.

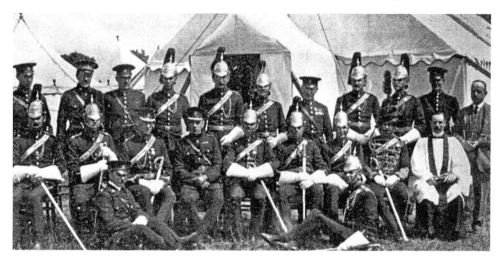

The yeomanry officers attending training at Colchester in 1913, taken by Ernest a'Beckett of Church Hill.

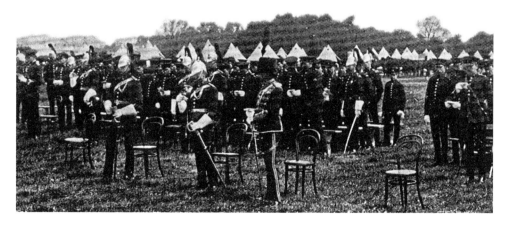

Church parade at a yeomanry camp in Colchester taken by Ernest a'Beckett.

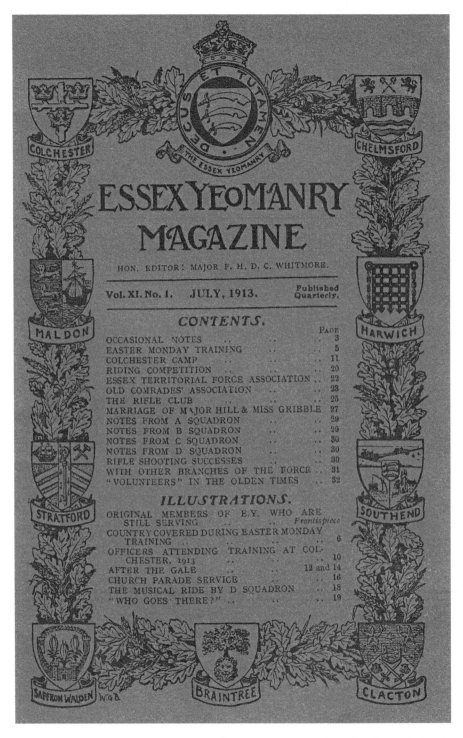

ESSEX YEOMANRY MAGAZINE

HON. EDITOR: MAJOR F. H. D. C. WHITMORE.

Vol. XI. No. 1. JULY, 1913. Published Quarterly.

CONTENTS.

ILLUSTRATIONS.

The practice of war games in the forest was a common event, and one local man had military connections. *The Essex Yeomanry Magazine* for July 1913 had a number of photos taken by Ernest a'Beckett of Church Hill.

They would often put on shows to display their horsemanship. The men had to perform a certain number of drills annually and the orders were issued in the *Essex Yeomanry Magazine*. Loughton and Walton Abbey troops had to report to Chingford in April 1912. The drills took place at weekends but there would also normally be a summer camp for a longer period of drills. There was another Loughton connection in the *Essex Yeomanry Magazine* of July 1913: all the photographs in the magazine were taken by Ernest a'Beckett of Church Hill.

There was an advertisement in *The Times* of December 1914 for the Volunteer Corps Officer Training Corps aimed at schoolboys over the age of sixteen and adult men able to do squad and company drill. They were invited to join a Christmas training camp at High Beech. Anyone interested had to let the caterer, Mr William Riggs at High Beech, know. The camp cost £1, which included three meals a day. There were to be carts available at Loughton station to carry baggage. Sleeping was to be indoors on straw and everyone had to bring their own blankets and towels. Rifles were not needed but a few ranging rifles and trenching tools would be useful. A miniature rifle range owned by Gerald Buxton had been loaned to the camp and a field to practise trench digging.

Braeside in Connaught Avenue was used as a military hospital during the First World War. It wasn't unusual for large houses to be taken over during the conflict. The hospital

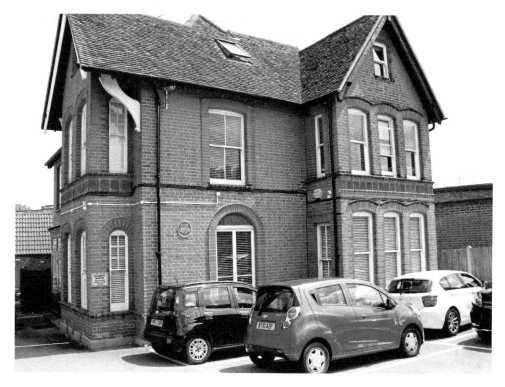

Braeside in Connaught Avenue was a First World War Red Cross Military Hospital, as the Blue Plaque on the wall shows.

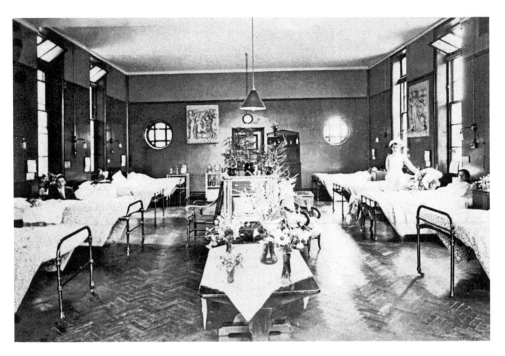

This is a postcard of a First World War military hospital. According to the card it was situated in Loughton Hall. It was common for large houses to be used as hospitals at this time.

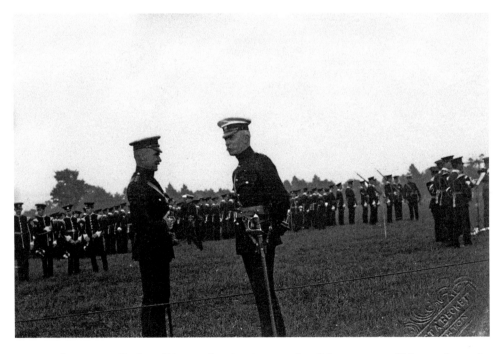

It seems that Ernest a'Beckett did not only take photographs of the yeomanry. This one shows the Essex Regiment in the First World War.

opened in January 1915 with fifteen beds and was mainly run by the Essex 36 Volunteer Aid Detachment. It was affiliated with Colchester Military Hospital and treated eighty-four patients in its first year. The number of beds increased until it had thirty-three by the time it closed in 1919. The building was then used as a school but later changed its name to Godiva House and is now used for offices. A Blue Plaque commemorating its use as a hospital was erected in 2012.

The wounded men of the war became a common sight in the town. Seats were placed outside the Crown Hotel where the men would sit and chat to the locals. Although the war may have seemed far off there was some evidence of the conflict when the first German airship to be shot down, by William Leefe Robinson, based at Hornchurch, was witnessed by locals. The airship came down at Cuffley.

Many literary and artistic people settled in Loughton, and another was to move close by during the First World War. Edward Thomas is remembered as a war poet, although many of his poems were actually written about Essex while he was based there during his service in the Artist Rifles officer training corps before he even got to the front.

It was while he was based at Romford that he spent some time on a training camp in Epping Forest. (I suspect that this was a retreat near Wellington Hill, which later became a youth hostel.) It had previous military connections as the man who ran it, William Riggs, had served with the yeomanry in the Boer War and enlisted in the First World War despite being fifty years of age when it began. The retreat was taken over by the War Office and was used as a training centre by the Artist Rifles.

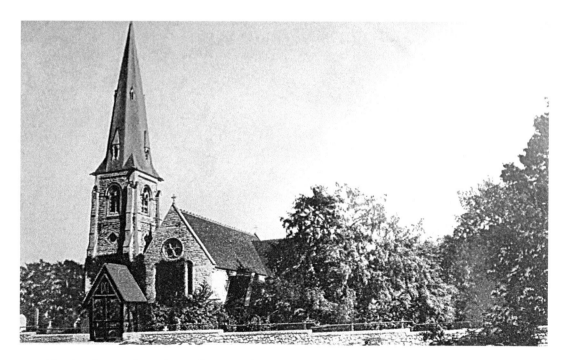

The church in High Beech is still surrounded by the forest and is more rural than the churches in Loughton.

Thomas loved the area so much that he found an old nurseryman's cottage near High Beech and moved himself and his family in – the previous tenant was already serving at the front. It was easier for Thomas to visit his family there when he could get away from Romford.

Thomas's wife Helen remembered living at the cottage, which she described as being in a terrible condition. Despite this they were often visited by other literary figures while living there. Thomas would take his children on walks through the forest, dropping white pebbles to find their way back, telling his children that they were like Hansel and Gretel. Thomas spent his last leave at the cottage at Christmas 1916. He then left and went to France where he was killed by a shell at Easter 1917.

It wasn't only the better-remembered local inhabitants that died during the war. Albert and Ellen Jackson lived in Forest Road and they had ten children, seven of them sons who went to fight in the First World War. The youngest of their sons was killed in action and two more of them later died of their wounds. The Jacksons received a letter from King George V saying how proud Mrs Jackson must have been.

It wasn't only the enemy bombs that were a danger to the local population during the Second World War. In 1941 an anti-aircraft shell fired at an enemy plane landed in the High Street, killing three people – one of them a policeman and another a local councillor.

Loughton was the site of one of the first fatalities of the war when a bomb fell near The Drive. This was in July 1940, and an auxiliary fireman was killed near an air-raid shelter in the Drive. A woman was also killed in a house opposite the shelter. The bombs did not always cause serious damage. One that fell in the fields in River Way left a large crater that the children used as a swimming pool.

During the bombing of London the residents of East London would bravely make their way to the safety of Epping Forest where camps were set up for them. They are said to have numbered in their thousands, which was a fact that the government were not keen to publicise at the time. There were parts of West Ham where the streets were so empty due to the population moving out that the army used the area to train in street fighting.

Loughton was very close to part of the defences against air attack on London. RAF Chigwell was just across the fields from Loughton on the site that is now a nature reserve between the River Roding and the M11. It wasn't aircraft that flew from this RAF station, however; it was barrage balloons. When enemy aircraft dropped bombs on the balloons they often landed on the houses of the Roding estate.

The servicemen and women from the balloon establishment were a common sight in the area. Many of them used the Kings Head in Chigwell as their local. As well as the balloon establishment there was also a hand grenade range between River Way and the river. This wasn't even fenced off.

As well as bombs landing in Loughton there were other dangers. In September 1940 a Hurricane was shot down and landed on a shelter in Roding Road, killing all those inside. The pilot was Polish and had ejected from the aircraft and came down safely. It was thought that he was German and he was arrested, an incident that seemed to happen quite often during the war to pilots from other parts of the world flying for the RAF. Members

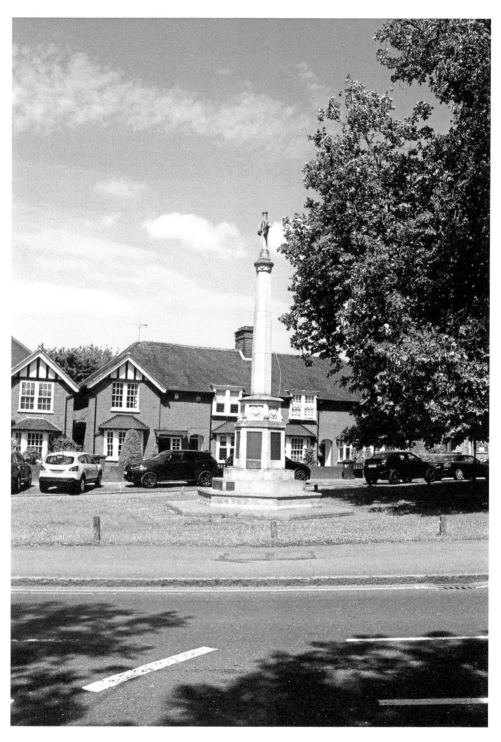

Loughton War Memorial stands on King's Green. It was unveiled in 1920 and has ninety names of soldiers who served in the First World War and sixty-four of those who served in the Second World War.

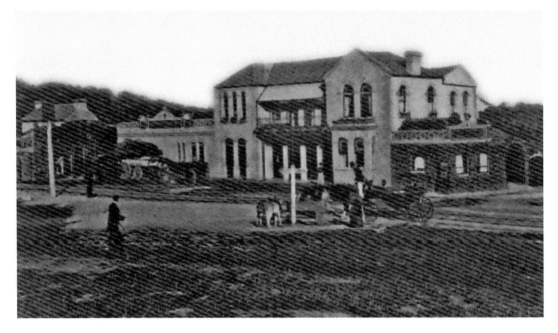

The Robin Hood is one of the older public houses in Loughton. It stands at the western end of the town.

of the Home Guard were often ready to suspect anyone coming down by parachute to be a German invader.

Another incident that was kept quiet by the government was when one of the first V-2 rockets fired by the Germans landed in the Epping area in early September 1944. The press were keeping quiet about this new weapon – the explosions were reported as being from ruptured gas mains. The secret was not well kept, however, as Londoners were talking about 'flying gas mains'. It was two months after the first rocket fell that the truth was revealed.

There was another close connection with the enemy when prisoner of war camps were opened in Cheltenham Gardens. There were two camps: one for German prisoners on the left-hand side of the road and one for Italians on the right. The Germans would often work outside the camp and were good builders. The Italians did not seem to be as popular; however, the prisoners held here were initially allowed more freedom than the Germans after Italy joined the Allied forces, though that changed as the war came to an end.

The end of the war did not stop the training of troops; as late as March 1954 battle games were still taking place in Epping Forest. According to *The Times*, the lovely forest between Loughton and Theydon Bois was alive with troops, guns and vehicles of war.

A battle group had moved by road from various locations in London. They had been called out by bugles following an order by the Prime Minister that all home-based troops – including clerks, cooks, batmen and general duty men – as well as those in combat training should be ready at all times to defend their own stations, or other key points. The men who were more used to being in ceremonial dress for their stations at Windsor were present in armoured cars rather than on horseback.

A brigade headquarters was set up in a country club at Abridge. It was guarded by the military police and although the cooks were part of the combat force, they put away their rifles to cook meals for the men. They once received word that parachutists had dropped near Cold Hall Wood. The commander, Brigadier R. Anderson, said afterwards that it had been carried out in a generally satisfactory way, except that wireless communication had left something to be desired.

6. Local Events

There was a local custom to hold a hunt in the forest at Easter, which was attended by numerous people from London. In April 1811 the Epping Stag Hunt was reported in *The Times*. It seems that a stag was caught before the hunt and then used in it. According to the report, the stag was captured after two day's pursuit near Loughton. It was then, according to manorial custom, turned out near the Bald Faced Stag public house for the diversion of the foresters and all comers. The stag had been brought to the site in a cart, and there were numerous horsemen assembled to enjoy the chase. There were hundreds of what were described as 'Cockney Nimrods' mounted on either their own strong-backed ponies or one obtained from the circulating studs of the livery stables. There were even more people assembled on foot – men, women and children.

The stag was released and ran down High Beech Hill, and was followed by a pack of dogs minutes later. They were an ill-matched pack, gathered together from various parts of the country, described as being scared of both the stag and the crowds. The pack dwindled in size as the chase went on and many of the riders fell off their mounts, while their horses carried on the hunt.

The stag kept to the grounds of the hill near the ponds behind Loughton, but was finally caught and carried to the Horse & Wells tavern at Woodford. The report said that the stag was plucked almost bald so the victors could decorate their hats with trophies of its hair. The hunt had lasted two hours and there had been no serious injuries, apart from the stag, which did not seem to matter.

There was an important visit in June 1880, when the Duke of Connaught paid his first visit to Epping as the Ranger to the Forest. The Duke, along with other dignitaries, travelled by train to Forest Gate, from where carriages took his party across Wanstead Flats and the entire southern section of the forest to Chingford. The Duke then opened a new road from Chingford to Loughton, named the Rangers Road. He went on to visit Loughton Camp, which, according to rumours at the time, was known as Boadicea's Camp and was where she was supposed to have fought her final battle against the Romans. After a visit to Baldwin's Hall, the Duke returned to London by a special train from Loughton.

Due to their location in the countryside, what was going on in London may often have passed the inhabitants of Loughton by. This was not the case though when the Royal Albert Dock was being built in 1886, which was achieved by blasting the ground. It was reportedly achieved with little noise – no more than that produced by the firing of a single cartridge. However, a Mr P. Gellantly from Loughton wrote to *The Times* on 26 April saying that the explosion from the docks was distinctly heard in Loughton and actually caused the windows in his house to shake.

There was a terrible accident at the Gunpowder Mill at Waltham Abbey in May 1894. Explosions were not uncommon during the period that the mill was in operation as the production of gunpowder was a risky business, but this one had fatal consequences. According to *The Times*, fragments of four men were found 600 yards from the scene of the explosion. The accident also had an effect on the Loughton area, where the sound was clearly heard. Windows were broken at High Beech School and some of the children were cut by flying glass. The windows of Loughton's Robin Hood Inn, 3.5 miles away from the mill, were also broken.

On 15 August 1926, a very unusual event occurred: earth tremors were felt in many parts of the country. Although the tremors occurred nationwide, no damage was sustained. It was described as a twisting or rocking sensation, and some people were shaken about in their beds. One resident of Debden Green reported a severe shock at around 4.45 a.m., which he thought was due to an explosion at Waltham Abbey Royal Gunpowder Factory.

An event took place in September 1931 that may sound comical to someone who wasn't there, but must have been very frightening to anyone who was. A bull was being driven from a meadow at Goldings Manor – the residence of Lord Stanmore – when it broke free and ran down the High Street. It then went into the offices of a local auctioneer, trampling on desks and furniture, chasing the occupants out, and causing at least £10 worth of damage, which I suppose would have been more if it had entered a china shop.

The bull was recaptured and put into a field with another bull. It then escaped a second time and was chased around the town once more: into the front garden of a house and then into the post office yard, where it stayed. The other bull was brought from the field, which lured the escapee out of the yard for it to be recaptured. It was then discovered that the second bull had also escaped, and was later found about a mile away.

It is hard to believe today that less than 100 years ago there were people who had to get their drinking water from ponds. This happened in the areas around Loughton in August 1935, when a number of water sources dried up. It seems that the council had been working through the winter to supply water to outlying areas, but it had been unsuccessful. Things were very bad in Ongar, where one family said that the well they normally got their water from had dried up. They had removed the weeds and scum from the top of a pond and dipped underneath for water. They strained the pond water several times, and boiled it, but it still tasted terrible.

In March 1955, an unusual event occurred that was connected with Loughton Carnival. At Edmonton County Court the treasurer of a charity fund was held responsible for a debt the carnival incurred. A summons had been taken out by Essex Steel Scaffolding of High Beech Road for the recovery of £38 17s 6d, the cost of hiring and erecting scaffolding for Loughton Carnival week. The summons was issued to Cyril Cramphorn of Roydon Close, Loughton, and secretary of the Chigwell Recreation Playing Fields Fund – the organisers of the carnival. Mr Cramphorn stated that he was acting on the fund committee's instructions in making the contract. Further summonses were issued against Mr K. Magnus of Dagenham, the treasurer, and Mr J. Eccles, the chairman of Loughton. However, Mr Eccles was ill in hospital at the time and so the summons against him was dropped, and Mr Cramphorn said that he did not sign the contract on his own behalf but on that of the organising committee. The judge said that it was ironic that Mr Cramphorn had not been in favour of signing the contract but had been overruled by the other officials. He had, however, legally made himself liable by signing it. The judge then said that the next charity he organised should be for the benefit of the secretary.

Bibliography

Addison, Sir W., *Epping Forest: Its Literary and Historical Associations* (J.M. Dent: 1945).

Addison, Sir W., *Epping Forest: Figures in a Landscape* (Robert Hale: London, 1991).

Brandon, D., *Stand and Deliver* (Sutton: 2001).

Calder, A., *The People's War* (Pimlico: 1969).

Green, G., *Epping Forest Through the Ages* (1996).

Green, G., *My Life in Loughton* (Loughton and District Historical Society: 2004).

Morris, R., *The Powell's in Essex and Their London Ancestors* (Loughton and District Historical Society: 2002).

Pearson's Weekly (May 1935).

Whiting, A., *The Loughton Roding Estate* (Loughton and District Historical Society: 1998).

Wilkinson D., *From Mean Streets to Epping Forest* (Loughton and District Historical Society).

Also available from Amberley Publishing

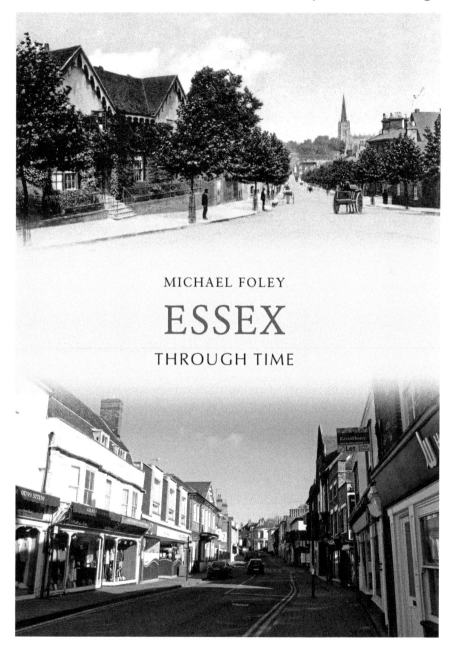

MICHAEL FOLEY

ESSEX

THROUGH TIME

This fascinating selection of photographs traces some of the many ways in which Essex has changed and developed over the last century.
978 1 8486 8618 2
Available to order direct 01453 847 800
www.amberley-books.com

Also available from Amberley Publishing

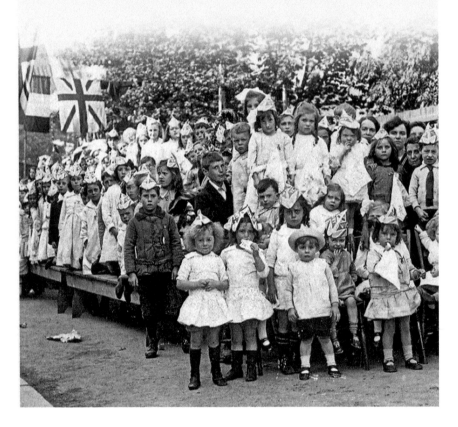

MICHAEL FOLEY

ESSEX AT WAR

From Old Photographs

A charming collection of wartime photographs of Essex.
978 1 4456 0991 1
Available to order direct 01453 847 800
www.amberley-books.com